DIY Hydroponics

101 hydroponic beginner's guide to building your indoor and outdoor complete gardening system. Learn step-by-step how to grow herbs, vegetables, fruits in your own garden. Start Growing.

THEODORE MONCANTO

Contents

WHAT IS HYDROPONICS

The term hydroponics, hydro - water and ponos - work, that is, work in water, was first used in 1940 by Dr. William Frederick Gericke, from the University of California. He developed a cultivation technique without soil where fruits, cereals, flowers and tubers were grown on a large scale and presented a work in which he researched the physiology, nutrition and growth of plants. He refined the technique and defined a name for this science.

Hydroponics is a technique or science used to grow plants without the presence of soil, transferring the nutrients that the plant needs only through an enriched aqueous solution, which will provide support for its development. This water will be a balanced solution, rich in nutrients, with the presence of elements such as nitrogen, phosphorus, potassium, among others, according to each plant species. There is strict control of the pH and concentration of nutrients so that the vegetable grows in the best possible conditions. The technique is also adapted according to the region where the plants will be grown due to climatic differences, water scarcity or lack of nutrients.

Non-mineral nutrients like carbon, hydrogen, and oxygen come from water and atmospheric air. Macronutrients such as phosphorus, calcium, magnesium, sulfur, and micronutrients such as chlorine, manganese, and iron are acquired by the roots. Thus, plants in hydroponics have their roots suspended at approximately one meter from the soil in an aqueous medium rich with the necessary nutrients for plant growth.

In addition, there are ways to practice hydroponics. The roots can be suspended in a liquid medium or supported on an inert substrate.

Hydroponic plant cultivation is an innovative cultivation technique in which plants are grown in a protected area (greenhouses and greenhouses with heating), without soil and exclusively in water , which allows the cultivation of plants throughout the year. It is a method that prevents the consequences of growing on poor quality soil. In this case, there is no need for soil sterilization and crop rotation . Planted plants do not come into contact with pests and diseases, so less money is spent on protective equipment, and more care is taken about the environment, which is especially true in a closed system where excess nutrient solution is collected in the tank and reused.

The hydroponic method of cultivation was first realized in 1930 at the University of Berkeley in California, but it was recorded long before that in the Babylonian gardens where the plants were grown on water.

The basis of hydroponic cultivation is the cultivation of plants in water during which the roots are laid in a solution of nutrients that is responsible for the growth of the plant. Oxygen must be present in the solution. When the root receives a nutrient solution, it very quickly absorbs oxygen and nutrients which affects the growth of the plant.

In hydroponic cultivation there is a difference in the system of irrigation , ie wetting of the substrate, and considering that they are divided into:

Open systems (drain to waste) - the nutrient solution is used only once, and after moistening the substrate, it flows out

Closed systems - the nutrient solution circulates in a closed system and is recycled. After irrigation, it is returned to the troughs where it is controlled and water and nutrients are added if necessary. These systems are the most acceptable because they are economical and environmentally friendly and save water by up to 70 percent

The largest leader in hydroponic cultivation is the Netherlands, followed by Australia, Canada, Japan, Malaysia, and the United States. In Croatia, too, there are more and more people who engage in this method of production. Hydroponic cultivation most often grows tomatoes, lettuce, cucumbers, peppers, spinach , cabbage, chicory , beans, new potatoes, asparagus , leeks, eggplant, carrots and other vegetable crops.

HISTORY OF HYDROPONICS

Hydroponics is currently considered a modern practice, but the cultivation of plants in containers above the ground has been attempted at different times throughout history.

The murals found in the temple of Deir el Bahari seem to be the first documented case of plants grown in containers (Naville, 1913). The mature trees were transferred from their country of origin to the king's palace and then cultivated in soilless cultivation when the local soils were not suitable for the plant. Many ancient civilizations have used above-ground cultivation for their agricultural production. In Egyptian hieroglyphic drawings dating back several hundred years, BC shows the cultivation of plants in water. The floating Aztec gardens used for certain cultures. The Hanging Garden of Babylon is also a good example of above-ground cultivation.

The oldest publication on above-ground cultivation was the book Sylva Sylvarum published in 1627 by Francis Bacon, and after that, water cultivation became a popular research technique. In 1699 John Woodward published his experiences of growing water with spearmint. In 1859-1860, the discoveries of German botanists Julius von Sachs and Wilhelm Knop led to the development of the technique of soilless cultivation. This cultivation technique quickly became a standard of research and teaching, which is still widely used and currently considered as a type of hydroponics.

In 1929 William Frederick Gericke Berkeley publicly promoted this crop as a solution for agricultural production. Gerick grew tomatoes twenty-five feet tall in mineral nutrient solutions rather than the soil. He also coined the term hydroponics in 1937 for growing plants in water (from the Greek hydro, "water," and ponos, "work"). One of the first successes of hydroponics was at Wake Island, where hydroponics was used to grow vegetables for passengers. In the 1960s, Allen Cooper in England developed the technique of filming nutrients. The Pavilion grounds at Walt Disney World's Epcot Center opened in 1982 and is prominent among the different types of hydroponic techniques.

During the 1960s and 70s, commercial hydroponics farms were developed in Abu Dhabi, Arizona, Belgium, California, Denmark, Germany, Holland, Iran, Italy, Japan, the Russian Federation, and other countries.

During the 1980s, many automated and computerized hydroponic farms were established around the world. For the past several decades, NASA has conducted extensive hydroponics research for its Controlled Ecological Life Support System or CELLS.

Plants: development and propagation

A fact of biology: Without plants, there would be no life on earth. Because it is the plants that both produce vital oxygen for us and serve as a basis for food. If there were no more plants to eat, herbivores would first die out, followed by carnivores.

The plant: development, structure, and nutrition

Plants develop from seeds. This is a kind of small nucleus that contains genetic information about the structure of the plant and some nutrients for initial development. Dry seeds can usually be kept for a longer period of time. Under certain circumstances, however, the plant will begin to germinate. Common germination criteria are:

1. It is moist around the seed, so it must be supplied with water.
2. Oxygen is present, and there is
3. a certain temperature. Each plant seed has a slightly different demand for its environment. The seeds of rice only start to germinate at around 10 degrees, while the rye in our fields begins to grow at around 2 degrees.

If the conditions for growth are favorable, the seed's shell is broken open, and the young plant begins to grow. The root anchors itself in the ground while the stem penetrates towards the surface of the earth. Four organs develop, especially in plants: root, sprout, leaves, and flower.

The root has the task of anchoring the plant in the ground and supplying it with water and minerals. While the root is below the earth, the plant continues above the earth through the shoot - often also called the stem. Branches from which the leaves hang from the shoot. So it should be clear: In order to supply the leaves with water and minerals, these supplies must be absorbed through the roots and delivered to the leaves through the shoot. The plant can breathe through the leaves, water evaporation takes place here, and stored substances are built up.

We would particularly like to go into the function of the stomata here. These are very small pore openings on the leaves of the plant. This can regulate its water balance, depending on the weather and humidity. One thing should also be understandable: the plant permanently absorbs water through its roots, which must flow somewhere, after all, the plant should not burst. It is necessary to release water again through the stomata. The plant also absorbs carbon dioxide through the stomata and is able to convert it into oxygen.

Plants: propagation

We have now dealt with how a seed becomes a plant. Now, of course, the question still arises: where does the seed come from? Well, plants have so-called stamens, which consist of a style and the anthers. In warm weather, the dust bags burst, and pollen is released. Sperm cells develop in the pollen grains, the male part for reproduction.

If bees and bumblebees are out and about on warm days, they discover the colors of the petals and fly to the plants to get nectar. While the bees and bumblebees fetch the nectar, small pollen grains stick to their hair. If the animals continue to fly to the next flower, they transport the fertilizable sperm cells to the female part of the plant, where pollination (successful fertilization) is possible.

The female part of the plant? Yes, you read that correctly. The female part of the plant is a kind of hollow in the middle of the flower. There is a carpel that looks like a stamp (and is therefore also called). The elongated part of the stamp is called the stylus; the upper part is called the scar. The thickened part is the ovary, in which there are ovules and egg cells for fertilization.

Root

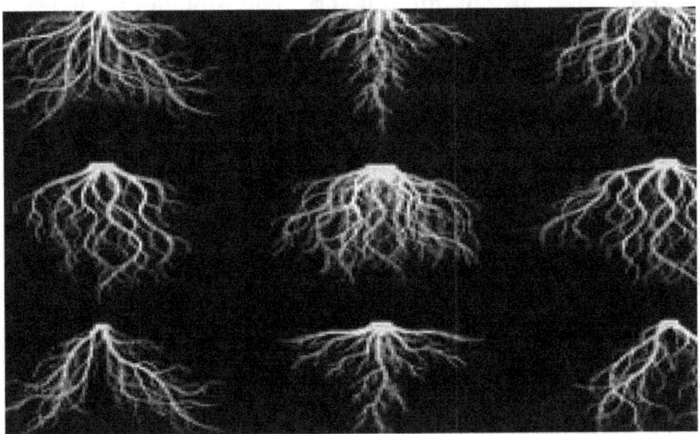

Do all plants form roots?

No, by far, not all plant species from a root system. However, it applies to those plants with which the hobby gardener has to deal most frequently, namely the so-called cormophytes. The plants in this group, to which all seed plants, club moss plants, and ferns belong, are constructed essentially identically: under the earth, the root grows, from which the shoot axis grows and on which leaves and flowers sit.

What are roots?

In addition to the shoot axis and leaves, the root (radix) is one of the main organs of the above-mentioned group of plants. It consists of a root cap (calyptra) and coarse and fine root hair. Coarse roots form the stable structure of the root structure, fine roots with a diameter of less than one millimeter are only small in size and have a long lifespan, but they play an important role in nutrient absorption. The structure of the root is extremely complex and consists of a large number of individual layers. The root can grow both in length and in width (secondary growth in thickness). The total surface of the root system in well-grown plants is often many times larger than that of the above-ground shoot system.

Drives out a plant, the seed root forms first and only then the shoot axis. Branches of the roots always arise from within (endogenously). In addition, roots never have leaves. Roots are positive gravitropic, which means that they always move towards the center of the earth as they grow, while the stem axis grows in the opposite direction (negative gravitropic). This is necessary so that the plant can assume an upright position in the substrate. According to the latest research, roots even react to light stimuli that are directed into the root system via the shoot axis, and in this way, adapt the root growth optimally to the needs of the aerial parts of the plant.

THE TASKS OF THE ROOTS

Roots fulfill many tasks for the plant. The absorption of nutrients and water from the environment is particularly important. Young fine roots are particularly active here - they supply the plant with minerals and liquid from the surrounding substrate. The older the roots become, the more they cork up and ultimately serve only for further transport, but can no longer absorb ions themselves. For this reason, a distinctive system of fine roots is essential for healthy plant growth. Damage to the fine roots, for example, due to waterlogging or over-fertilization, results in severe supply shortages on the plant. For a better absorption capacity, the root systems of the plants often enter into symbiosis with fungi and bacteria from the soil. In addition to the exchange of nutrients, own chemical compounds are also synthesized in the root. Various plant hormones and secondary plant substances are created within the root. The third important function of the plant root is to anchor the shooting thing firmly in the ground. Roots are always attached "on the move" - the holding power of a healthy root system is enormous.

Shallow or deep root?

Root systems can be both heterogeneous and homogeneous. A heterogeneous root system consists of a large, vertically downward growing primary root of the first order and a network of smaller secondary roots of the second and third-order branching off from the main root. Homogeneous root systems, on the other hand, consist of many roots of equal rank, which hardly differ from one another. Whether a plant is rooted flat or deep in the ground depends not only on its type but also occasionally on the surrounding soil conditions. There are three basic types of root patterns in garden plants: deep root, shallow root, and heart root. Deep roots like fir and oak usually have a tap root and penetrate deep into the ground in search of groundwater. Flat roots, such as spruce or willow, on the other hand, spread their roots evenly around the stem axis in the horizontal direction and supply themselves primarily with seeping surface water. Heart roots such as beech and linden are a mixed form, the roots of which grow in all directions and adapt flexibly to the soil conditions.

SPECIAL FORMS OF ROOTS

In addition to the classic root systems, there are a variety of other forms of roots that have arisen through metamorphosis. These transformations represent a specialization of the root in a special living environment.

Storage roots: In particular, taproots like to use their roots to store reserve materials there. This is very pronounced in beets (for example, sugar beet, carrot) and root tubers, such as those found on dahlias or the celandine (Ranunculus ficaria), the case. Even water can be collected in the storage roots. This process is called water succulence. Over time, a well-watered green lily forms thick, white storage roots. Warning: bulbs and tubers are not storage roots, but parts of the leaves and shoot axis of a plant that have been converted to store nutrients!

Climbing, stilting, and support roots: Where a particularly secure attachment of the plant is necessary, special roots are often formed in addition to the supplying root system, which gives the plant better hold. Various climbing plants use their root tendrils (vanilla) or sticky roots (ivy) to pull themselves up against walls, fences, or other plants. Corn plants need support roots, which prevent the narrow, tall plants from tipping over. Mangrove trees and some plants near the bank, such as the screw tree (Pandanus), form stilt roots, which lift the shoot axis out of the surrounding, usually watery or swampy substrate.

Aerial roots: aerial roots are a specialty of epiphytes, which, like many other species of cactus, orchid, and bromeliad, belong to. This group of plants can also absorb water and nutrients through roots that grow above ground, because the elevated position of the plants, which gives them a greater yield of sunlight and rain, means that the roots usually do not reach down to the ground. Some types of aerial roots are even able to do photosynthesis instead of leaves.

Rhizomes: In the true sense, rhizomes are not roots, but an underground extension of the stem axis. Rhizomes are always the same length because growth and degeneration are always in balance. Every year new rhizomes emerge from the rhizome on the surface. The rhizome serves both as a nutrient depot and as a vegetative reproductive organ of the plant.

Pull roots: This particularly strong type of root ensures that bulbs and tubers, but also rhizomes, do not migrate to the surface of the earth over time. Roots exert a strong downward pull and hold the soil rung attached to them in place.

What should be considered when planting?

Depending on the root system, gardening needs differ in care. While flat roots are dependent on regular watering due to their root system lying close to the surface, deep roots usually survive long dry periods without any problems, since they cover their fluid requirements in deeper layers of the soil. Flat rooters spread their roots in a plate shape around the shoot and thereby compete with other roots with flat roots. Make sure there is sufficient planting clearance here. Deep roots - especially those with a strong taproot, sometimes many meters long in trees - can penetrate underground pipes and even concrete sewage pipes and damage them.

Taproot likes to settle on dry, deep soil as well as in cracks and crevices. Flat rooters, on the other hand, prefer loose, humus-rich soil without waterlogging. While deep-rooted plants are extremely storm-proof, flat-rooted plants can be torn out of the ground together with root balls in heavy winds. Plants with a homogeneous root system (all roots are of equal rank) offer particularly good erosion protection and are suitable for stabilizing slopes, for example. Plants that reproduce through root runners (e.g., bamboo) should be planted with a rhizome barrier as a precaution to prevent uncontrolled spreading.

AQUAPONICS

Aquaponics is a combination of hydroponics and aquaculture.

Aquaponics uses the water from the fish tank, which circulates through a culture bed where the plants are grown. Nitrifying bacteria convert fish droppings into available plant nutrients. Plants use these nutrients for their main nutrient intake. The water is filtered by plants, giving the clean fish water to live in. With aquaponics, fish and plants thrive in symbiosis in an almost autonomous mini-ecosystem.

Is aquaponics organic?

The aquaponics is totally organic. Plants and fish contribute to the aquaponic cycling process with the fish providing the plant nutrients and the plants that filter the water to make the fish feel good.

The only inputs that you will have to provide are fish food and sometimes some natural additives such as rock powder, chelated iron, or algae.

Is it reserved for professionals or individuals?

As small-scale aquaponics is rather simple to practice, there are more and more private amateurs who use it to grow food and fish for their families.

There are installations of individuals of all sizes but also commercial aquaponics installations, even aquaponics factories. An aquaponic system can be adapted to an aquarium that is already running or can be started from scratch, you see.

Note that the commercial aquaponics industry has been developing very quickly in France, all the more since the push towards the use of more sustainable means of agriculture has started since the last episodes of drought and the beginning of the crisis. Some hydroponic and aquaculture companies have converted their existing businesses to aquaponic systems, and other companies have implemented aquaponics systems from scratch.

Should outdoor aquaponics be practiced in a greenhouse?

In reality, it all depends on your climate. A greenhouse is not an essential part of an aquaponics system, even if it provides enormous protection for the system against exposure to the weather (rain, hail, wind, etc.).

If you stay in an area where it freezes in winter, a greenhouse is necessary for the protection of fish and plants during the colder months. Your pools must be frost-free. Aquaponics systems can also be set up indoors, using horticultural lamps and neon lights on plants instead of using sunlight. This system uses more power than a conventional system exposed to the sun due to the cost of operating the lights, but it is sometimes the only one possible in certain periods.

WHAT ARE THE ADVANTAGES OF AQUAPONICS?

There are many advantages to practicing aquaponics. Among these many advantages, here are the main ones:

- Reduction of water consumption from 90 to 95%
- Plants grow 3 to 4 times faster than in soil.
- No need to use chemicals and fertilizers; everything is organic.
- Reduces the use of pesticides
- No need to bend over to cultivate, the culture tanks are at breast height.
- Reduced operating costs compared to conventional horticultural operations.
- Back-breaking work like digging the ground and weeding for the gardener

Can produce fish and plants for family/producer all year round, growing under glass or indoors

Compared to conventional hydroponic crops, aquaponics does not need to use chemical nutrients for plants, since fish droppings provide these nutrients for plants. This eliminates the pollution of rivers, which is usually used in aquaponics. No salts are rejected.

Compared to conventional aquaculture producers, an aquaponics system does not have an accumulation of waste in the system, which causes toxicity due to nitrites. Aquaponics uses this waste, along with the bacteria in the beds, to develop the transformation of nitrites into nitrates, which plants consume as the main source of nutrients.

Aquaponics can be practiced on polluted soils because there is no contact between plants and the soil.

HYDROPONIC BENEFITS FOR EVERYONE

Healthier and stronger daughter plants: The plants grown with these systems generate healthier and stronger daughter plants than the ones grown in the traditional way; therefore, there will be a progressive improvement of the cultivated species.

Natural selection and optimization: Each plant species requires environmental and nutritional characteristics that will determine its development.

In hydroponic systems, it is possible to recreate them in order to allow the chosen species to develop to the best of its ability.

Control on the nutrient solution: It is possible to control and manage the supply of nutrients that will reach the roots of the plants through the water at any time.

Water saving: In these hydroculture systems, there is no waste of water, all that consumed refers to what is actually necessary for the plant for its growth, therefore no dispersion in the soil.

Fertilizer savings: the plants will absorb the received nutrients, and the sextants will remain in the water, which will continue to feed the hydroponics quindi no dispersions as for the water.

No pesticides or almost: Under the optimal conditions reproduced in the hydroponic system, the species will grow in a healthy and rapid way; this will allow a pest-free growth in most cases, and in any case, to deal with the possible pest in a selective and less aggressive way.

Maximum yield

No herbicide: In the pots, there is only room for the plant we grow, so there will be no need to weed and consequently, not even to pollute.

Excellent yield: Being able to nourish and grow in an ideal environment, the species will enjoy excellent health and will produce more fruits and better, larger, rich in vitamins and flavor.

Root control: Being immersed in the nutrient solution and not in the soil, the roots can be easily inspected, this allows to identify any pathogens early and to intervene promptly and with greater and more efficacy, especially for the cultivation of medicinal plants in which the substance useful is found precisely in the root system.

Biomass: Plants grown in hydroculture have a very abundant vegetative phase thanks to the high nitrate content in the nutrient solution, which is very useful when biomass is needed for various uses, from composting to fuel production.

Extreme conditions: Just think that hydroponic modules are used by NASA for space missions to feed astronauts. these systems can integrate everything needed for plant growth, including the rays useful for chlorophyll photosynthesis.

It is obviously not necessary to have extreme situations, but these systems improve and reproduce every nutritional and environmental aspect necessary for the optimal growth of the plant.

We value space

Little space: Thanks to the high efficiency and the right nutritional contribution, the plants will not need to compete for survival, therefore the root system will be much less developed than the plants grown on the ground.

This allows to have a very high cultivation density per square meter, even in the order of 100 units, obviously based on the upper part of the same.

Little physical work: Enough heavy bags, hoe, lawn mower and various tools. Physical work is minimal, as well as production waste, this makes hydroponics the perfect system even for those who live in the apartment and have very little space.

Versatile and productive: Another aspect to be taken into consideration is the different need for nutrients of the various species in the various growth stages, therefore it will be possible to cyclically use a solution used for a type of plant for a phase of its development and then pass it to a another that needs it in a subsequent period simply by changing the container of the nutrient solution.

NUTRIENTS FOR PLANTS: WHAT DO PLANTS NEED TO LIVE?

NUTRIENT AND WATER INTAKE

Depending on the type of plant, the required nutrients are taken from the soil, water, or air. Plants usually take simple inorganic compounds such as water (H 2 O), carbon dioxide (CO 2), nitrate (NO 3 -), phosphate (PO 4 3-), potassium (K +), sodium (Na +), sulfur (S 2), Magnesium (Mg 2+), etc. We do not want to write a treatise for chemistry students here, but to bring garden enthusiasts closer to the needs of their plants. Therefore we keep the explanations a bit simpler:

CORE NUTRIENTS

Light and photosynthesis

A very special substance is found in the leaves of the plants: chlorophyll. This green dye not only gives the leaves and plants their rich green color but is also responsible for the fact that plants are able to convert carbon dioxide, water, and salts into glucose with the help of sunlight. The plant then also excretes oxygen as a waste product. As long as plants get enough light, they grow uniformly and regularly.

If there is a lack of light, however, plants grow much faster in the desperate search for more light - the plant "hurts." While the plant is striving for rapid length growth, root growth, chlorophyll production, and leaf growth are put on hold. The structure of the parts of the plant that have grown too quickly is also not particularly stable. Such plants will often remain sickly for a long time and take a long time to regenerate. For this reason, you should never start growing vegetables such as. starting from tomatoes.

If there is a lack of light on one side, e.g., if one side of the plant is shadowed by another, larger plants, the plant will try to grow away from the oversized shade. You should always ensure there is sufficient clearance and an appropriate location so that the plants in the garden are always well supplied with the light.

The importance of water for the plant

Especially in the dark months, many plants do not have enough sunlight. If you don't just want to use plants that need little light and brightness, you can put a plant lamp on its own. However, there are also several differences in the field of lamps, especially for plants.

The main criterion is: where should the lamp be installed? Point two: what performance should it be? The type of plant plays a role in this because some needless and a little more light. If you prefer vigorous growth and want large flowers, you should generally choose 60 watts per square meter for lighting.

ADVANTAGES AND DISADVANTAGES OF PLANT LAMPS

Before purchasing, the user should be informed of the scope and lamp type. Empholes are mostly daylight lamps that suggest the special light as well as possible. The lamps are based on natural sunlight and are destined for the delivery of the plant in question.

Daylight plant lamps guarantee average sunlight and sufficient light. The trade offers lamps from 650 to 5,400 lumens. Experts do not always advise against this type of lamp, although the plants feel comfortable under it.

The reasons are obvious because the lamp is more expensive than conventional daylight lamps, and some people find the light color extremely uncomfortable. They are, therefore, less suitable for a normal living space. The advantages are that they provide plants with sufficient light and ensure better growth. The disadvantage is the significantly higher power consumption.

Others are enthusiastic about LED lighting. They are currently the most powerful light source, emit precise radiation, and are also energy efficient. LEDs have a positive effect on plants because they grow better and better.

Artificial light for houseplants

Plants need light so they can grow and bloom. However, if there is not enough sunlight, the owner should help with a plant lamp. However, not all of these lamps achieve the desired success, but for photosynthesis, only certain spectral light ranges, namely violet-blue and orange-red, can be used.

Photosynthesis is important for the growth of a plant. The supplied light energy is used to produce the water, carbon dioxide gas, glucose, and oxygen that plants need for healthy growth.

Depending on the type of plant, the light requirement varies, some need a lot of light (approx. 16 hours a day), others less. Especially in the winter months, the amount of natural daylight is not sufficient.

If you don't know, the leaves of the houseplants turn pale green, later change color to yellow, then brown. Eventually, they fall off completely and go to the trash. With suitable LED lighting, a plant gets exactly the light it needs, and healthy growth is guaranteed.

Advantages of LED plant lamps

- The plant uses the violet-blue and orange-red light spectrum for photosynthesis
- The lamps are characterized by long life and low heat development
- Plants thrive faster and more evenly
- LED comes from English and means "light-emitting diodes." Not only are they very energy efficient, but they also have a very high light output. They are, therefore, ideally suited to give houseplants the right light.

Pay attention to safety criteria.

Security plays an important role in your own home. Of course, this also applies to plant lamps. When buying an LED plant lamp, there must be adequate ventilation in the foreground. It must either be installed in the lamp or have passive ventilation.

Another quality feature is a series connection with different constant current sources. This aspect prevents too much voltage from occurring after only one LED has given up the ghost, and not all of them fail in succession.

Anyone who has discovered online shopping for themselves should be particularly careful when buying. LED products must be a reputable supplier, and there must be a minimum two-year warranty.

Overview of different plant lamps

Illumination source:	Advantage:	Disadvantage:
Incandescent / halogen lamp	very inexpensive	too much red, not suitable for plants, strong heating by infrared radiation
Plant lamp based on incandescent lamps	inexpensive	absolutely unsuitable for plants, too low efficiency, inappropriately expensive
Fluorescent lamp	high efficiency, low power consumption, low heat generation	no continuous spectrum, too weak in the red range
Special plant fluorescent lamp	high efficiency, low power consumption, low heat generation	Light color often not pleasant, can only be used to a limited extent for living rooms

Special plants - fluorescent lamps

These lamps are very expensive, and the light consists only of red and blue waves. There are no medium green waves. The advantage of the lamps is that they offer optimal lighting conditions and have a pleasant effect on the human eye. However, the light is only moderately useful for living rooms.

A commercially available fluorescent tube is suitable as a commercially available alternative. It offers excellent plant light as it mimics the spectrum of sunlight. It also doesn't get too hot and is readily available.

Make artificial plant lighting yourself.

If you are planning to build your own system lighting, there are a few things to consider when planning. The main point is the selection of a suitable place. It should be noted that there is a power source nearby. At the same time, this area should be protected from possible moisture.

The proximity of the facility is also an important aspect. The principle to be observed here is that a distance of 15 centimeters from the system must be maintained for every 6 watts of lamp power.

Note how long the plant is exposed to light. A timer is recommended, but a certain rhythm needs to be developed. Like humans, plants need a rest phase to recover from photosynthesis.

However, growing new shoots from seeds requires a certain base temperature. LEDs are hardly suitable for this. They would not be enough to generate enough heat, and an additional heat source would have to be installed.

The green thumb for a nice house

Outside, the sun provides flowering and green plants. It is not always easy in a closed room, but it is possible with special plant lamps. However, conventional lamps are hardly suitable because they do not meet the special requirements of indoor plants.

Plants do not necessarily depend on the brightness of light but on the different color spectra. For healthy growth, they mainly need the colors red and blue in a ratio of 8: 1 to 3: 1, depending on the plant type and growth phase.

The exact color spectrum is provided by special plant lamps, which are available in energy-saving LED technology. They consume little electricity and contain no toxic mercury. In addition, the long lighting duration is undisputed.

LED lamps are ideal for perfectly illuminating places with little light, growing plants, and spending the winter successfully. There are also some reasons to choose an LED plant lamp.

- No additional equipment like a reflector
- low acquisition costs
- long life
- No additional device required

Reasons for an LED plant lamp

The new technology makes this type of plant lamp very efficient. They do not generate heat that would be lost when not in use. They can be placed directly above the system as they do not generate any heat. The lighting works efficiently with a small footprint.

In order to grow optimally, plants need not only the right light but also the right temperature. If the environment is too hot, photosynthesis is not correct. If it's too cool, it won't even start.

Conclusion: The plants irradiated in this way become stronger, bigger, and healthier. It is completely independent of the seasons and the lighting conditions outdoors. Other factory lamps use up to 80 percent more energy, which protects not only your own wallet but also the environment.

An LED lamp with different radiation distribution is for sale, depending on the place of use and for which type of plant. The key is the red, yellow, and blue components. Green does not contribute to photosynthesis since plants do not absorb this color error.

AIR - CARBON, OXYGEN [CO 2 / O 2]

Plants also have to breathe. Plants growing on land have small stomata on the underside of the leaf, through which they absorb gases and moisture from outside. During photosynthesis, the plant needs carbon dioxide from the air and releases oxygen (light amination). In the dark, the plant needs oxygen and releases carbon dioxide.

THE IMPORTANCE OF AIR FOR PLANTS

Humidity

Plants absorb water through the roots, which evaporates through the leaves through the heat of a grow light. In this way, plants 'sweat' and the air in a grow room becomes increasingly humid. By allowing air to flow past the leaves, it expels this moist air and replaces it with new, drier air. This allows the plant to absorb more moisture (and fertilizers) from the soil. This moist air discharge not only ensures faster juice flow and growth but also significantly reduces the risk of mold.

Two major enemies of plants are spider mites and flying bugs, such as the fungus gnat. These insects love stagnant air. In it, they can fly around undisturbed and crawl without drying out.

However, they have a much harder time when disturbed by wind and drought. Moreover, due to good air circulation and removal of warm moist air, the top layer of the earth remains dry, which makes laying eggs for these insects more difficult.

Spider mites, especially to this extent a huge source of stress for plants (and the grower). Good air management significantly reduces the chance of these annoyances!

Fans

Swinging fans are by far the best to control good air circulation. If you don't have room for a swing fan, you can also use a regular table fan, but a moving fan prevents the wind from always being directed to the same spot.

The goal is good air circulation around the foliage of your plants; you achieve this by aiming the fan just above the plants. In this way, it sets the plants in motion and dissipates heat under the lamp. Don't put your fan in a storm setting, but make sure you have a gentle breeze. Preferably do not aim it full on a plant, just above it. Make sure that all branches and leaves move slightly in the wind.

Suction

The capacity of an extractor is indicated in cubic meters per hour. This is the number of cubic meters of air that the extractor can move in 60 minutes. Based on that capacity, you can calculate which extractor is best suited for your grow room.

Extractor capacity in cubic meters = (grow space) x 5 x 60

In view of the heat, choose an extractor that can move the air content of your grow room at least 3 times in a minute. It is useful to have some overcapacity as the outside temperature varies in summer and winter. With a so-called fan controller, you can then control the suction power of the extractor manually or automatically so that the temperature remains nicely stable.

For example, if your grow tent has a capacity of 12.5 cubic meters (2.5 x 2.5 x 2 meters, content = length x width x height), you will need at least one extractor that will charge 37.5 (3 x 12) every minute. , 5) can move cubic meters of air.

Tube or snail shell?

There are two types of extractors, tube fans, and cochlea fans. Tube fans are a bit cheaper than cochlear fans. They are also a little easier to install because they do not have to be built in a box and are actually the first choice for a small grow room, such as a tent or a cupboard. Tube fans generally make a bit more noise because they have no conversion. They also usually have less capacity than cochlear fans. There are also tube fans for sale with a built-in thermostat to properly regulate the temperature.

Snail shell fans need to be built in a box, which makes them a bit more expensive than tube fans. They are, therefore, a bit quieter, especially if you do not let them run at maximum speed. Not all fans are dimmable, ask the store which one is if you want to dim your fan. It is useful to have a dimmable fan because then you can adjust the extraction to the needs of the plant.

If your fan makes too much noise, you can first hang it from rubbers. This dampens the vibrations and thus the noise. Many box fans (built-in volute fans) already come with such suspension rubbers. There are also silencers for fans available. You mount them at the outlet, and you can make a whisper-quiet extraction with it.

Drain

When choosing an extractor, you must also take into account the resistance of air hoses with bends and, for example, your carbon filter. All resistance to this type of matter increases the required capacity of your extractor. Fortunately, for a small grow tent or cupboard, it is sufficient to exhaust the air in the room where the grow room is located.

If you go bigger, it is better to discharge the air in another room. For example, you can choose in an adjoining room where a window is ajar. Or you can exhaust the air from your grow room through an existing flue such as a chimney.

WATER - HYDROGEN, OXYGEN (H 2 O)

As we all know, living things need water to live - plants would dry up without water. Depending on the type of plant, water is taken from the ground, from the air or from raindrops on the surfaces of the plant. With aquatic plants, the water can be absorbed all around the plant. Plants on land usually absorb water through their root hairs. The water is transported up through the stem axis via bundles of ladders into the leaves, flowers, and fruits. Dissolved nutrients are also absorbed with the water. The water evaporates again through small stomata in the leaves. The water serves as a means of transport and solvent for nutrients, and it also plays an important role in photosynthesis.

If there is a lack of water, the internal cell pressure (turgor) drops, and the plant leaves the leaves hanging and soon begins to wither. As there is usually only a small amount of CO2 in the air, the stomata are opened wide during photosynthesis (see section »Air«). Depending on the ambient humidity, the plant can lose large amounts of water due to evaporation (perspiration). If there is not enough water from the roots, the plant will quickly become limp and wither. So to save houseplants a high water loss, should be for a sufficient humidity be taken care of. An exception is, for example.

There may also be excess water if, for example. The irrigation water remains in the pot. A lack of water is usually tolerated better than a surplus of water since standing water in the pot or oversaturated soil can cause the roots to suffer from a lack of oxygen and to rot.

Where it is and what it is used for

Water is contained, in variable amounts, in all plant tissues, and then in all cells.

Water is present in the soil as a solution in which mineral salts are dissolved, and in this form, it is absorbed by the roots.

From the roots, the solutions rich in absorbed substances reach all parts of the vegetable thanks to a system of conducting vessels.

In the physiology of plants, water has an irreplaceable function because all vital reactions are possible only between dissolved substances.

The substances processed in the synthesis processes, such as photosynthesis, are gradually dissolved in the circulating aqueous solution, and this is how they can then reach all parts of the plant, thanks to other conducting vessels, to feed them.

Water allows enzymes to perform their irreplaceable action in the processes of cell turnover and is used for the accumulation functions of reserve substances, such as potato starch, which can be converted into sugars as needed, following reactions of hydrolysis where water is needed.

Cell multiplication is possible only if there are adequate quantities of water inside the cells, which are rich in both plasma and cell wall levels. The high presence of water in the cells that constitute the most active organs in the growth processes, the vegetative apices, can be observed, especially in spring when the buds sprout, tender and easy to break.

The water, which is abundantly present in the cells, gives turgor and mechanical consistency to organs that do not have supporting tissues, such as grass stems.

It also allows, thanks to evaporation, that the aerial parts of the plants do not heat up too much when the sun beats, and the ambient temperature is high.

The lack of water leads to the withering of the plant, a state of suffering that can be temporary if the plant quickly finds the amount of water necessary to restore normal metabolism, or permanent when this does not happen, and the normal metabolic reactions can no longer take place. In this second case, it is an irreversible state, which leads to his death.

The vital nature of water is also evident when observing the behavior of quiescent organs such as seeds: they can be stored for very long periods if kept in a dry environment, they are again able to germinate in the presence of water.

How much there is

The percentage of water present in plants is variable.

The stems of some plants in arid areas, such as cacti, contain up to 97-98% of their weight and constitute real living stocks. A thick cuticle and the leaves transformed into quills allow reducing evaporation and perspiration to a minimum.

On the contrary, the seeds are usually the vegetable parts that contain very little (the mustard seeds 7%, the castor seeds 6%), a characteristic that guarantees their long shelf life.

Nitrogen (N)

Plants need nitrogen primarily for the growth and formation of leaf mass and leaf green. A simple system for classifying plants according to their nitrogen requirement is the categorization into heavy, medium, and weak consumers.

An excess is shown by particularly dark green plants, long, thin, and weak shoots and spongy plant tissue. It shows itself in the form of weak growth (dwarfism) and small leaves and poor rooting. The leaves turn evenly light to yellow, starting with the older leaves. The fruits of such undersupplied plants are also smaller. As a result of the nitrogen deficiency, the absorption of other substances such as phosphorus, potassium, magnesium, and other trace elements is restricted.

Nitrogen is contained in compost, nettle slurry, leaves, horn shavings, horn meal, and feces from herbivores, for example.

Phosphorus (P)

For example, phosphorus is contained in leaves and poultry manure. An excess is shown in growth disorders.

A deficiency leads to weak growth, weak root growth (roots often turn reddish), small flowers (poor flower formation), and leaves as well as leaf tip drought. Starrtracht: The leaves turn blue-green to violet on the underside; the top turns brownish, bluish, or in "dirty" green.

Unfortunately, it has been shown that in many gardens, the lawn is mostly heavily over-fertilized with phosphorus from artificial fertilizers, but most other nutrients are lacking. This can easily happen with blue grain or green grain, for example. Laypeople, in particular, damage the plants but also the soil through incorrect fertilization or over-fertilization.

Phosphates are contained in compost, nettle slurry, comfrey slurry, horn meal, or horn shavings, for example.

MAIN NUTRIENTS

Potassium (K)

Potassium is important for the regulation of the water balance, the strengthening of the cell tissue, the increase of frost hardiness (winter hardiness), and the aroma formation of fruits and vegetables. Potassium also promotes root and tuber formation as well as shelf life, which is particularly important for carrots and celeriac, for example.

One recognizes a deficiency, despite sufficient watering, quickly withering or weakly growing plants. Older leaves turn yellow from the edge and dry. The taste and shelf life of fruits and vegetables are reduced. Lacerations and tears in radishes, kohlrabi, and tomatoes (tomatoes) can occur more easily. In the case of fruit trees, the leaves roll up; the leaf edges are dry and brown.

An excess is noticeable through inhibited growth and can cause root burns and the death of plants.

Contain potassium in compost, rock flour, nettle liquid manure, liquid manure comfrey, Farnkraut Jauche, algae manure, cattle manure, poultry manure, and wood ash and beech wood charcoal.

Calcium (Ca)

Calcium raises the pH of the soil (it deacidifies the soil) and has a positive effect on the ventilation and crumbliness of the earth. Calcium also improves the availability of other nutrients. Calcium also controls the stomata of the leaves, strengthens the cell walls (the plant tissue), and stimulates cell division and soil life.

An excess of calcium can be recognized, among other things, from leaf chlorosis. Too much calcium (e.g., in irrigation water) traps iron, potash, copper, boron, zinc, magnesium, and phosphorus. The leaves turn yellowish-green over time. This can often be observed with potted plants. Especially in the case of azaleas, citrus plants, camellias, and gardenias, you can see the leaves turning yellow when the water is too calcareous. An excess of calcium can also lead to the death of young plant parts, caring flower buds, and roots that remain small.

Calcium is contained, for example, in compost, nettle slurry, comfrey slurry, eggshells, or wood ash (beech charcoal).

Magnesium (Mg)

Magnesium is the most important building block of leaf green (chlorophyll), the regulation of the entire water balance of the plant, and is necessary for the formation of protein.

A deficiency can be seen in small fruit. Older leaves become spotty and light to yellowish while the leaf veins initially remain dark and green. The leaves can turn brown from the edge and dry. There is a reduced root formation. Magnesium deficiency can often be observed in conifers, for example. For larch, pine, or spruce. Conifers get yellow or brown needles or even brown tips. In the end, the affected needles fall off. This often occurs on heavy, loamy, and lime-poor soils or with unbalanced fertilization.

An over-fertilization of magnesium can lead to calcium deficiency.

Magnesium is contained, for example, in compost, nettle slurry, comfrey slurry, Epsom salt, algae lime, and partly in stone flour and in wood ash (beech charcoal).

Sulfur (S)

Sulfur occurs in a wide variety of forms in nature, and emissions from industry and transport also release sulfur. Plants are usually always adequately supplied with sulfur. In many artificial fertilizers, but also e.g., There is a lot of sulfur in horn shavings. An over-fertilization can lead to acidification of the soil quickly. In the rare cases that a plant suffers from sulfur deficiency, this can be recognized by thin and woody stems and young leaves with a light yellow color.

Included is all the same whether they now come in many sulfur fertilizers from nature or the chemical plant. A lot of sulfur can be found, for example, in horn shavings, nettle and leech, and leech.

Trace nutrients

Trace elements or trace nutrients such as iron, copper, boron, zinc, manganese, and molybdenum are only required in small quantities. There are also other nutrients that are known to be beneficial to plant growth, such as aluminum, sodium, chlorine, silicon, and cobalt. These substances are often considered dispensable, but strictly speaking, the importance of these substances for plants cannot yet be scientifically explained.

All kinds of these elements and others occur in healthy soil, and it has been sufficiently researched which substances plant process in which way and what some of these substances are needed for.

MINERAL NUTRITION OF PLANTS

Plants obtain from the external environment the substances necessary for the biochemical reactions of vital processes. Sunlight, water, and mineral elements present in the soil are indispensable for plant life. The soil is composed of an aggregation of particles whose electronegative colloids or electropositive colloids attract positively charged cations or negatively charged anions, important for the mineral nutrition of plants. There are some elements considered essential for the life of plants, as they are implicated in the fundamental metabolic processes of all plants. For example, calcium, which serves to regulate the permeability of cell membranes, is considered an essential element, as no plant could live without it.

Each element considered essential for the growth and biochemical processes of the plant meets three requirements:

- it must be necessary for the completion of the life cycle
- it must be necessary for itself and cannot be replaced by other elements
- it must act inside the plant and not outside

The essential elements can be divided into macronutrients and micronutrients. Macronutrients are those elements necessary in large quantities for the life of plant organisms, while micronutrients, despite being required in very small quantities, are essential for the development of plants throughout the crop cycle. Nitrogen, phosphorus, potassium, sulfur, calcium, magnesium are considered macronutrients. We call micronutrients: iron, boron, manganese, copper, zinc, molybdenum, chlorine, and - in traces - nickel.

Nutrients

Most of the mineral elements present in the soil derive firstly from the mother rock and organic matter and, secondly, from the wind, rains, and surface water.

The elements necessary for plant nutrition can be found in the soil in different forms:

- as constituents of soil minerals (K, Ca, Na of feldspar, pyroxenes, etc.). They are not readily available, but become so with the alteration of minerals;
- combined in complex forms, very stable, poorly soluble. They can be assimilated only if degraded in other forms;
- dissolved in the soil solutions in ionic form. Readily assimilated;
- absorbed by soil colloids, which, having negative (humus, clays) or positive (hydroxides of Fe and Al), are capable of fixing cations ($Ca2 +$, $Mg2 +$, $Na +$, $K +$, $H +$, etc.) or anions ($PO43-$, $SO42-$, $HCO3-$). These ions are called exchangeable because reversibly exchanging with the ions present in the soil solutions; they can be absorbed by the plants.

Exchangeable ions are a very important source of mineral elements for vegetation, as they are released into the soil as plants require it; moreover, this mechanism removes them from the risk of runoff, which would lead to the depletion of the soil.

Soil acidity

The availability of mineral elements in the soil depends on the degree of acidity of the soil itself. The degree of acidity is known as pH and has values between 0 and 14. The closer we get to zero, the more we say that the soil is acidic; on the contrary, as we get closer to 14, the soil becomes more and more alkaline.

The pH regulates, through the cation exchange of the ions, the solubility of the different salts of the soil, and, therefore, the availability of nutrients for the plants. Among the main exchangeable ions, the cations that prevail in neutral and alkaline soils are, in order: calcium, magnesium, potassium, sodium, and ammonium. In acid soils, the most abundant cations are hydrogen and aluminum. In neutral soils, however, we find iron, zinc, and phosphorus more easily. The optimal pH is that in which all the necessary elements are available in maximum quantities and have values generally between 6.5 and 7. The competition between the various species of plants has, over the course of evolution, determined the different adaptations of the plants under different soil acidity conditions.

Today we can say that there are species that prefer acid soils and others that adapt better to alkaline soils. In particular, the so-called "acidophilic" plants such as camellia, gardenia, rhododendron, and azalea are best found in acid soils. On the contrary, plants like lettuce, onion, and beetroot live better in soils with a pH between 6.5 and 7.5. Finally, carrot, pea, strawberry, and tomato are best suited to soils with pH 5.5-6.5. For example: if we grow an azalea on alkaline soil, it will easily show iron deficiency symptoms, as this element - more abundant in acidic and neutral soils - has a very low concentration in alkaline soils. For this reason, on the market, we often read on packages of potting soil or "specific for acidophilic" fertilizer,

IMPORTANCE OF SOIL STRUCTURE IN AGRICULTURE

The soil is the place where plants grow; it is an ecosystem formed by well-differentiated parts that constitute the structure of the agricultural environment, being the basis for the life of plants and a fundamental source of nutritive elements. These parts can be divided into 3 fractions:

The solid fraction made up of mineral elements (sand, clay, silt, limestone) resulting from the disintegration and alteration of the bedrock and organic matter resulting from the decomposition of plant and animal remains. The liquid fraction of the soil, in which soluble organic and mineral substances are in solution.

The gaseous fraction made up of gas from the air in the atmosphere, the life of microorganisms, and the gas produced by the decomposition of organic matter.

In short, agricultural soil is composed of minerals that serve as food, soil that retains moisture and microorganisms, which help it retain its good properties.

The physical factor has special relevance in intensively cultivated soils.

Having an oxygenated soil, with good structure and balanced in its nutrients is optimum for the farmer, and in this way being able to obtain good yields. If the soil is poor, does not have adequate acidity, or is damaged in structure, crops are unlikely to prosper even if the climate, labor, and irrigation accompany them.

The degree of acidity of a soil is measured according to its pH, which ranges between 0 and 14. If the pH is 7, it will be a neutral soil; below; it would be acidic soil, and above, alkaline. The ideal soil would be neutral, although most plants tend to alkaline for better mineral absorption.

When a loss in the vigor and productive performance of the plants begins to be detected, this may be due to the sowing of a certain crop repeatedly on the same soil, appearing what is usually called "soil fatigue," with a large number of chemical, biological and physical factors that can, more or less jointly, trigger this fatigue.

The physical factor has special relevance in intensively cultivated soils. Water is the main factor involved in the breakdown of soil aggregates, and this destruction can occur through different mechanisms, the direct impact of raindrops or irrigation being the most important.

When the soil begins to give problems, and we realize that the yield of our crop decreases, we can use different soil recovery techniques, but the two most common and effective are the following:

Whitewashed. Many farmers have to apply lime directly to the soil to correct the excess acidity of their soil; in any case, it is always a good idea to do a soil type analysis first. At first glance, the acidic soil is darker and tends to puddle, the alkaline has a very light color, almost whitish, and is usually rich in nutrients.

Manure. It is the perfect remedy to restore health to the soil, it acts as a filter for the soil, favors the root and obtains a good protein for the plant, significantly increasing productivity and providing multiple benefits to the soil, which can be summarized below:

- **Physical benefits**: Prevents soil compaction, increases water retention, reduces erosion, reduces waterlogging, improves resistance to frosts, and intense summers, favoring root development.
- **Chemical benefits:** Detoxifies plants by excessive use of chemicals, provides all the elements and microelements, acting as a pH corrector in acidic soils and as a salinity corrector.

- **Biological benefits:** As the soil is a living being, compost provides great biological richness, and mitigates the impact of pests and pathogens.

HOW SOIL IS DIVIDED AND ORGANIZED

Soils and their characteristics can vary spatially, both laterally and vertically. Vertical variability is defined by the presence of different levels with different characteristics and properties, forming a sequence of horizons that constitutes the edaphic or solum profile.

Therefore, the horizons are levels more or less parallel to the surface with characteristics that differentiate it from the others but are related.

Soil begins to form when a rock is exposed to the atmosphere, and it begins to be colonized by lichens and when its minerals begin to decompose and physically and chemically alter. This process is known as meterorization. This results in the formation of horizons A and C.

Horizon A: It is the most superficial horizon and is formed by biological activity as a consequence of the implantation of vegetation.

Horizon B: also called accumulation horizon. Its origin is a consequence of the processes of translocation and transformation of the materials of horizons A and B. In it accumulates products of alteration and new formation.

Horizon C: it is the deepest (located after B) and is made up of bedrock and fragments derived from weathering.

SOIL TYPES AND THEIR CHARACTERISTICS

There are several soil classification systems (Kubiena classification, French, Soil taxonomy-USDA, WRB-FAO / UNESCO), but recently, in 2006 FAO, ISRIC / World Soil Information and the International Union of Soil Sciences developed a new version of the World Soil Reference Base (WBR). Currently, it is the official soil classification system in the European Union and establishes the following types of soils :

Organic soils

Histosols: made up of little or no decomposed plant remains, with or without a mixture of sand, silt, or clay, in conditions of excess water. They typically appear in mobs or peat bogs. Soils conditioned by anthropic influences

Anthrosols: formed by land mobilizations, accumulation of rubble, residual sludge, or contributions of manure or with agricultural use.

Technosols: soils developed on manufacturing, construction, or mining waste.

Low evolution soils highly conditioned by climate.

Cryosols: they are permanently frozen (permafrost).

Low evolution soils highly conditioned by the original material.

Andosols: with a high content of amorphous or low crystalline materials from pyroclastic volcanic materials. They are found in almost any climate.

Arenosols: sandy soils.

Vertisols: very clayey soils.

Other soils of moderate evolution

Umbrisols: soils rich in organic matter and acids.

Cambisols: they are characterized by weathering of the parent or initial material.

Soils conditioned by topography and by water

Leptosols: they are very shallow soils on continuous rock and extremely gravelly and/or stony soils (lithosols).

Regosols: they are very weakly developed mineral soils.

Fluvisols: they are located near rivers and present a stratified profile where the amount of organic matter decreases irregularly or is abundant in very deep areas.

Gleysols: soils with water permanently (or almost) in the first 50 cm. There is a reduction in iron oxides, and they may have reddish, brownish, or yellowish colors or also grayish/bluish.

Stagnosols: they are soils with a layer of water that allow intense reduction conditions, and due to the washing of the materials produced by the water, it can present albic or whitish horizons.

Planosols: they are soils with a light-colored surface horizon that shows signs of periodic stagnation of water that abruptly passes to a horizon with a significant increase in clay with respect to the surface horizon.

TYPICALLY ARID OR SEMI-ARID CLIMATE SOILS

Solonchaks: soils with a high content of soluble salts (halite, gypsum) and humus.

Solonetz: uncommon and have high proportions of sodium and / or magnesium.

Calcisols: soils with accumulations of calcium carbonate.

Gypsisols: soils with gypsum accumulations.

Durisols: soils with silica.

TYPICALLY STEPPE-LIKE SOILS

Chernozems: cold steppe environments. Dark brown or black surface horizon from the accumulation of organic matter and may have calcium carbonate in the deeper horizons.

Kastanozems: drier and warmer steppe environments. The surface horizon of chestnut color because there is less accumulation of organic matter.

Phaeozems: warmer and wetter steppe environments. Similar to the previous ones, but without calcium carbonate.

Soils with a rich clay subsoil

Albeluvisols: presents horizons with mineral depletion due to their elution by the passage of water.

Alisols: very acidic soils. In any climate excluding tropical and subtropical zones.

Acrisols: the advanced degree of weathering. Only in tropical and subtropical climates.

Luvisols and lixisols. They are similar, although they differ in the type of clays they present.

TYPICALLY TROPICAL AND SUBTROPICAL CLIMATE SOILS

Nitisols: deep, well-drained, red tropical soils with a clay subsurface horizon with sodium. Rich in iron.

Ferralsols: they are the classic soils of the humid tropics, deeply weathered and with red or yellow colors. They are usually clayey with a high content of iron and aluminum compounds.

Planosols: Soils with hardened crusts of clay, iron, and quartz.

PHOTOSYNTHESIS

Photosynthesis is the biochemical process by which plants convert inorganic matter into organic matter, taking advantage of energy from sunlight. This is the main nutrition process not only of plants but also of other autotrophic organisms endowed with chlorophyll.

It is one of the most important biochemical mechanisms on the planet since it involves the manufacture of organic nutrients that store the light energy of the Sun in different useful molecules (carbohydrates). So its name comes from the Greek voices photo, "light," and synthesis, "composition."

Subsequently, the synthesized organic molecules can be used as a chemical energy source to support vital processes, such as cellular respiration and metabolism.

To carry out photosynthesis, the presence of chlorophyll, a pigment sensitive to sunlight, is required, which gives plants their characteristic green coloration. This pigment is found in chloroplasts, cellular structures of various sizes that are characteristic of plant cells, especially leaf (leaf) cells.

The organisms capable of carrying out photosynthesis are plants (both aquatic and terrestrial) and ferns, algae, and certain types of bacteria-free life. They can do this in two recognizable ways:

Oxygenic photosynthesis, one that not only produces useful sugars for the plant but also consumes carbon dioxide (CO_2) and under produces oxygen (O_2).

An oxygenic photosynthesis, one that does not produce oxygen (O_2), but uses sunlight to break hydrogen sulfide (H_2S) molecules, releasing sulfur into the surrounding environment or accumulating it within the bacteria that are capable of carrying it out.

This gas exchange is fundamental for the ecosystem and for life as we know them since it allows the creation and circulation of organic matter and the fixation of inorganic matter. Furthermore, oxygenic photosynthesis is essential for respiration, which works by exchanging gases in reverse.

PHOTOSYNTHESIS CHARACTERISTICS

Broadly speaking, photosynthesis is characterized by the following:

It is a biochemical process of obtaining organic materials, that is, of synthesis of nutrients, from inorganic elements such as water, CO_2, or nitrogen.

It can be carried out by various autotrophic or semi-autotrophic organisms, as long as they have the chlorophyll pigment. It is characteristic of plants, trees, ferns, algae, phytoplankton, and different bacteria. Only a few animals are capable of photosynthesis, including the sea slug Elysia chlorotica and the spotted salamander Ambystoma maculatum (thanks to symbiosis with algae).

The first photosynthetic organisms are estimated to have emerged on Earth about 3.46 billion years ago.

It generally under produces oxygen, which is released into the surrounding medium, although there are also an oxygenic variants (not producing oxygen).

Photosynthesis is a chemical process that occurs in two different stages: light and dark, so-called because only the first one involves the presence of sunlight (which does not mean that the second occurs during the night).

Clear or photochemical stage, in which the bioluminal reactions take place inside the plant. It all starts when the chlorophyll molecule comes into contact with solar radiation, and the electrons in its outer shells are excited, triggering an electron transport chain (similar to electricity). With this energy and in the presence of water, two different molecules are then synthesized: ATP (adenosine triphosphate) and NADPH (nicotine adenine dinucleotide phosphate), in a process called photophosphorylation, and which can be acyclic (oxygenic) or cyclic (anoxygenic).

Dark or synthetic stage, this phase takes place in the matrix or stroma of chloroplasts, taking advantage of the molecules generated during the previous phase to synthesize organic substances through a chemical reaction circuit known as the Calvin-Benson Cycle. Using different enzymes and using carbon dioxide as well as various nitrate or phosphate, they can be synthesized various compounds of carbon, nitrogen compounds, or sulfur compounds, necessary for the maintenance and growth of the autotrophic organism.

IMPORTANCE OF PHOTOSYNTHESIS

As we said before, photosynthesis is a vital and central process in the global ecosystem for multiple reasons. The first and most obvious is that it saturates the atmosphere with oxygen, an essential gas for respiration in both water and air. Without plants, we would simply suffocate.

On the other hand, by absorbing it from the surrounding environment, plants help fix CO_2 in their bodies, converted into organic matter, freeing the atmosphere from their presence. This gas, which we breathe out as we breathe, is potentially toxic.

Therefore, the decrease in plant life on the planet affects the increase of this gas in the atmosphere, where it acts as an agent of global warming, that is, as a greenhouse gas, preventing excess heat from radiating out of the atmosphere. Each year, photosynthetic organisms are estimated to fix about 100 billion tons of carbon as organic substances.

How do light intensity and lighting duration differ?

In the course of the growth cycle, from cultivation, growth stage to flowering and fruiting, the light requirement of the plant changes, and the light saturation point shifts upwards as the plant grows, ie, it can tolerate more light without suffering from it. However, this relates above all to the light intensity and not to the lighting duration, because more leaves can simply convert a higher amount of light than less photosynthetic foliage. Since the chloroplasts work synchronously, the low light intensity cannot be achieved compensate by longer exposure time.

If the light intensity is increased, this only leads to an increase in photosynthesis if the addition of nutrients and the Co 2 content of the ambient air is increased at the same time. Light intensity and lighting duration should not be confused with each other.

THE DEPENDENCE OF PHYSIOLOGICAL PROCESSES ON LIGHT AND DARK

Water + carbon dioxide → glucose + oxygen + water

$$12H_2O + 6CO_2 \rightarrow C_6H_{12}O_6 + 6O_2 \uparrow + 6H_2O$$

At the beginning of the 20th century, the influence of the duration of lighting on the plants and, ultimately, photoperiodism was discovered by chance on a tobacco plantation.

Photoperiodism, composed of photo - light and period - a period of time, means the influence that the length of the day and thus the exposure time has on the growth and development of the plant. The dark phase is also always considered. Specifically, it is about the relationship between the two and its impact on plants.

The most prominent example is the induction of flowering by a certain length of night. In the process, short-day, long-day plants, and day-neural differentiated plants. Short-day plants start to bloom when the nights are of a certain length—long-day plants when the nights fall below a certain number of hours. In day-neutral plants, the light-dark ratio has no influence on the flowering induction. The dark phase required for short-day plants for flowering induction is not the same for all plants of this type. For some, even nighttime stray light from the moonlight is enough to prevent flower induction. Some plants need shorter days or longer nights to start flowering. A distinction is made between nights in spring and autumn.

Short-day plants include hemp, rice, bell pepper, beans, soybean, coffee, and long-day plants include rye, wheat, and potatoes. Tomato and sunflower are, for example, day-neutral plants.

That means, depending on the type of plant, the induction of flower formation can be specifically controlled by the duration of the artificial lighting. For each species, research must be carried out to determine the critical value to which the plant responds. Early flower induction naturally shortens the plant's vegetation cycle and enables earlier harvesting. Nevertheless, enough room should also be left for the vegetation phase so that a vigorous plant is created that can ultimately also bear heavy fruit.

Plants can "see."

Photoperiodism shows that plants can perceive light, and this is not only used for photosynthesis purposes. Rather, the light perceived by photoreceptors controls various processes in the cells of the plant. The specialized photoreceptors are stimulated by light of certain wavelengths, and ultimately gene expression is promoted or suppressed.

THE BIOLOGICAL RHYTHM

The biological rhythm describes regularly recurring physiological processes. When processes are adapted to the day and night cycle, one often speaks of the "internal clock" or circadian rhythm. There are processes that are triggered by external factors, such as photosynthesis, which can only take place under the influence of light, and endogenous processes that are initiated by the organism itself every 24 hours.

The processes initiated by external factors can be important for the healthy development of the organism. In plants, the 24-hour to be illuminated, the twilight and dark phase can operations in the plant by eliminating suppressed be. Daylight serves as a timer for the plant. With Cryptochrome, a photoreceptor for predominantly blue light, it senses when the day is. Phytochrome, on the other hand, notices when it is getting dark, and it is time to "sleep." They then regulate the gene expression of the plant. Phytochrome also seems to tell the plants when their metabolism has to switch to cellular respiration.

At night, as part of cellular respiration, the products of photosynthesis and the Calvin cycle are converted: glucose and oxygen to water, carbon dioxide (CO_2), and adenosine triphosphate (ATP). ATP is the cell's energy source. Water and CO_2 are removed from the plant. ATP is essential for an increase in biomass, i.e., the growth of the plant. Cell respiration also occurs in plants during the day but is surpassed here by the photosynthetic performance of the plant, which is why the oxygen release of the plant releases CO_2 during the day quantitatively exceeds. It is, therefore, clear that the plant does not only grow in the dark and that photosynthesis with its products and, therefore, but the light is also essential for cellular respiration. If the plant also breathes cells in bright light, the question arises whether a dark phase is necessary at all?

Growth spurt in the early morning

In the trial, plants added the most biomass in the early morning hours before dawn. At dusk, three proteins combine to form a protein complex that suppresses the expression of two growth genes. This protein complex breaks down again overnight so that growth occurs in the early morning hours since protein biosynthesis of the growth genes can start. The plant grows faster than during the day. The proteins resulting from protein biosynthesis are broken down again during the day.

Plant light - effect on a plant

Therefore, a basic understanding of how (artificial) plant light affects the individual plant and why it is vital for them is necessary.

The right light for the plants

For this, a plant needs water, carbon dioxide, and light. The light is absorbed with the help of chlorophyll, the green dye that gives the leaves their color. The glucose and the waste product oxygen are then produced from these three components.

The glucose then acts as a nutrient in this process; the oxygen is simply expelled and can then be inhaled by other living beings.

However, chlorophyll cannot absorb all types of light equally. The light is divided into three parts or light waves.

This classification of the individual light waves is called the spectrum. Because the white light, as it is generally known, consists of three colored waves on closer inspection, which form the basis for all other colors and merge seamlessly into one another.

The long-wave, red waves, the short-wave, blue waves, and the green waves, which are medium in length, are important for photosynthesis.

While the red and blue waves can be absorbed by chlorophyll, the green waves are only reflected. These are useless for the photosynthesis process.

The two aforementioned light waves have the following influence on the nutrient formation process. The red, long waves can be absorbed very well by chlorophyll, but due to the good processing quality, they can cause the plant to "hurry up".

This means that new shoots grow to enormous size at breakneck speed and can, therefore, no longer carry their own weight.

This can damage the plant, as these shoots usually simply snap off. It is also said that the red light encourages the plant to bloom.

If, on the other hand, you illuminate the plant with pure blue light, this has a little positive impact on the plant due to the low intensification options. The blue light should only affect the general growth, which is why lamps with exclusively blue waves are also referred to as growth lamps.

It is therefore essential for artificial lighting that either the lightwave spectrum of natural sunlight is imitated as faithfully as possible, or that the ratio of the red and blue light waves to one another is made as proportional as possible.

Which plant light is the right one?

There are different plant lights for each of these options, the respective advantages and disadvantages of which are briefly explained below.

The incandescent lamp, or halogen lamp, is cheap, but not useful for artificially lighting plants.

This lamp emits too much red. As already explained, this leads to the plant being healed. In addition, this illuminant heats up extremely, which can lead to damage to the plant due to the too high temperature, since the risk of drying out or burning, especially with sensitive plants, is very high.

The lamp manufacturers have tried to make this type of lighting suitable for plants and have developed a light bulb, especially for plant lighting. This has a separate red light filter.

This is intended to project the exact amount of red light waves onto the plant. However, these filters are usually not enough, and the plant is still illuminated with too much red light.

In addition, the heating of the incandescent lamp does not fail to materialize, and this lamp is also extremely expensive due to the built-in filter compared to the commercially available model.

The sodium vapor low-pressure lamp, on the other hand, is more efficient. This means that it uses very little electricity, and it does not heat up excessively. But this lamp is very expensive to buy.

It also sends yellow light waves, i.e., a balanced ratio between blue and green light waves, and therefore has a little positive impact on plant growth.

In addition, the lamp also requires a certain warm-up time after each switch. It is, therefore, not possible to switch them on again shortly after switching them off.

If you want to do without this heating-up time, you can use a high-pressure sodium lamp. But the purchase of this lamp is also noticeable in your wallet, and because of the similar range of lines as the low-pressure lamp, it only works slightly better than this.

Alternatively, a metal halide lamp with white light can be used. These copies the spectrum of natural sunlight very faithfully and, at the same time, does not heat up excessively.

In pure reference to the efficiency of this plant light, it is highly recommended. However, this lamp is also very expensive and requires a certain heating time.

The special plant fluorescent lamps are also very expensive. Their light is composed only of red and blue waves and therefore, completely dispenses with the medium-length, green waves.

Sodium vapor lamp

In this way, the optimal lightwave ratio is created, but it creates an unpleasant shade for the human eye. This light is, therefore, of limited use for living rooms.

The cheapest alternative is the commercially available cool white fluorescent tube. This is great for plant lighting because it mimics the spectrum of sunlight, does not develop excessive heat, and is easily available.

LED fluorescent tubes are, therefore, most suitable for growing plants at home. For example, the Osram brand offers them inexpensively but with high quality, which enables you to build an effective plant light yourself.

These are also inexpensive and also allow more targeted irradiation of individual plants.

Artificial plant light - the right use

If you now intend to produce a plant light yourself, some things must be taken into account when planning.

A suitable location must first be selected. It should be noted here that there is a power source in the vicinity. At the same time, however, this must also be adequately protected from the resulting moisture.

It is also important that the plant lights are placed in the right proximity to the plant. The basic principle here is that every 6 watts of lamp power should be kept 15 cm away from the plant.

Led Lamps

It should also be known how long the respective plant should be exposed to. A timer is recommended for this, and it should also be noted that the plant also develops a certain rhythm. She also needs the nightly rest phase from photosynthesis, comparable to human sleep.

However, a certain basic temperature is usually required for growing new shoots from plant seeds, which is why LED lamps are not practical in this case.

These hardly generate any heat during the irradiation, and an additional heat source has to be set up.

However, it should be considered in the warm and dry heated air that prevails in most households during the wintertime.

If possible, most types of plants must not be in the immediate vicinity of the heating. Here, too, the individual needs of each plant are in the foreground.

Different light colors

In order to artificially illuminate plants, the light that the plant uses in nature must be imitated. The so-called white light (sunlight) is perceived by the human eye as white but consists of different colors with different wavelengths. With the help of a prism, the white light can be broken down into blue light in the short-wave range, long-wave red light, and green light in the medium-wave range.

The red and blue light can be absorbed by plants, and the green light is reflected. In addition to the right illuminance, the mixing ratio of red and blue light is crucial for optimal plant growth. If the plant receives an excess of red light, it grows very strong and forms a lot of unstable new shoots.

Not every light source is suitable for plant lighting

To create the optimal growth conditions for plants, the trade has a wide range of artificial light sources.

Gas discharge lamps

Gas discharge lamps, also called fluorescent tubes, have a wide color spectrum and require a ballast. Standard tubes with "cool white" light are suitable for plant lighting because they are similar to sunlight. In addition, there are high-quality fluorescent tubes on the market, whose efficiency is higher. Because they deliver up to 25 percent more light with constant power consumption. Fluorescent tubes with so-called "warm white" light are less suitable because they provide too much red light.

Sodium vapor lamps

So-called sodium vapor lamps achieve a high light output and are used efficiently as artificial light sources. Especially to illuminate the plant in the flowering phase. Like the fluorescent tubes, you need a ballast.

Metal halide lamps

Metal halide lamps also require a ballast and are a full substitute for the sun. Their light spectrum lies in the blue and white range, which means that they effectively serve plants as an additional light source in the winter months. Since they do not provide red and yellow light, metal halide lamps can also be used in plants during the growth phase.

Led Lamps

In recent years, LED lamps have also established themselves as outdoor plant lighting. Due to the high absorption, very good results can be achieved with LEDs. They also work very effectively and use little electricity. LED lamps also have the great advantage that they can emit almost any light color in the color spectrum precisely.

Light bulbs

Ultimately, it should be mentioned that incandescent lamps are generally unsuitable. On the one hand, the efficiency is very low, and on the other hand, they hardly use the blue-violet light range.

Duration and intensity of lighting

Plants that do not hibernate come from tropical or subtropical areas. Such plants should be illuminated for about nine hours at a light intensity of at least 700 lux during the faint winter months.

Hydroponic crops. Journey through the most popular cultivation systems

One of the most popular hydroponic systems, widespread and used in the world of indoor and above-ground cultivation, is the drip system. Used widely by both home and professional growers, this type of plant is characterized by a limited number of components, has a rather simple structure, is easy to manage, versatile and effective.

As the name suggests, the hydroponic drip system works in such a way as to make the nutrient solution drip directly onto the roots of the plants present in the system by supplying them with water and nutrients. Ideal for crops of any size, the drop hydroponic systems are particularly suitable for plants that require large spaces at the roots and - more generally - for all plants that tend to grow much in growth.

A drip system is characterized by a large container, to be placed at the bottom, on the bottom of the grow box or in the room set up for cultivation, where the roots can grow, another container to store the nutrient solution, an air pump, for allow the solution to reach the roots of the plants, the channels, and the pipes to connect the pump in the tank to the plants and a timer to automatically activate the entire system.

How does a hydroponic drip system work?

The nutrient solution is pumped and pushed upwards from the bottom of the tank to the growth substrate, where the plants are placed, from which it drips onto the plants thanks to the special tubes equipped with drips and the excess liquid falls back to the bottom, thanks to the special holes, ready to be reused in the next irrigation session.

Another widespread hydroponic cultivation system is the DWC - Deep Water Culture, in which the plants are suspended high inside the grow box or grow room - thanks to a special structure - with the roots slightly immersed in a well-oxygenated, composed of water and nutrients.

This method is called Deep Water Culture for two fundamental reasons; the first is related to the depth of the tank and the amount of water present inside it: more water means more stability of the nutrient solution, which translates into less maintenance by the grower. The second reason is closely related to the irrigation method; if in most hydroponic systems the roots are periodically sprayed and are in contact with water only at certain times of the day, in Deep Water Culture, the roots of the plants are constantly immersed in a perfectly oxygenated nutrient solution.

The third most common hydroponic cultivation system among growers who opt for soilless cultivation is that which uses Nutrient Film Technique, NFT. Appreciated for its simple, easy to manage and particularly intuitive design, this system is particularly suitable and frequently used for small and fast-growing plants, such as lettuce varieties, but also aromatic herbs and small vegetables.

There are various possible versions for an NFT system, but all united by the presence of a constant flow of water that flows on a slightly inclined mat, covered with a film impregnated with nutrients: the water - in the flow - collects the substances and distributes them to the roots of the plants present in the system.

One of the disadvantages of this system is in need to always guarantee a constant flow of water, which - on the occasion of sudden power outages - would be interrupted, creating critical issues and compromising the growth of plants.

A NFT hydroponic system is composed of a tank for the nutrient solution, an immersion pump, pipes and channels, rockwool cubes, or small baskets in which to contain the seedlings and a return system, which is used to bring the nutrient solution from the irrigation channels to the tank.

Floating plants

They are very original aquatic plants, easy to grow, and very decorative. They can have roots planted in the earth at the bottom of the body of water or floating below the water limit. They have the characteristic of being able to survive and be cultivated at any depth of water. The floating plants have brightly colored flowers, sometimes with a pleasant scent and leave large. Depending on the species, floating plants can be very large and, therefore, suitable for decorating and embellishing large basins or bodies of water and other small or dwarfs suitable for small ponds.

Environment and exposure

The suitable environment for floating plants consists of more or less large bodies of water, ponds, reservoirs, etc. They prefer exposure in full sun, some species, the most delicate and sensitive ones, fear the cold and therefore, during the cold seasons, should be kept in warm places.

METHODS OF HYDROPONICS

What is deep water culture?

Deepwater cultivation is an active hydroponic system in which the roots of the plant are suspended in a nutrient solution. The plant is, therefore, always fed with water and nutrients.

Plants are in clean pots and are fixed with a substrate.

Net pots can be placed above the water surface in two ways: either drill holes in the lid of the water tank or place the net pots on a floating platform.

The latter variant has the advantage that the roots are always surrounded by the nutrient solution.

BENEFITS

Deepwater cultivation is one of the simplest hydroponic systems. In this system, the roots have optimal access to water and nutrients. That's why vegetables and herbs grow quickly and efficiently.

Three advantages make deepwater cultivation so popular:

- low maintenance
- fast and easy to build
- very efficient and profitable

Because of these advantages, the system is ideal for beginners and advanced users.

- downside
- The hydroponic system
- tends to lack oxygen and
- not suitable for all plants.

Since the nutrient solution does not circulate in the system, no oxygen enters the nutrient solution. The oxygen in the water is absorbed by the roots over time. Since the roots rot if the oxygen content is too low, the plant can die as a result.

Fortunately, with the help of a pond or an air pump for the aquarium, the danger can be eliminated: the air bubbles enrich the nutrient solution with oxygen and promote growth.

Build a deep water culture yourself

Now you know how the system works and what its advantages and disadvantages are. Great! With this, you are ready to build your culture in deep water.

For the basic system of deep water culture, you need:

- a water tank,
- Net pots,
- Substrate,
- a floating platform/cover e
- an air pump (optional).

So far, so good. Before you begin, however, keep the following tips in mind:

The water tank

Nothing beats a sturdy water tank. A simple box with a lid is the most suitable. The holes can be drilled in the lid and insert the pots into the net.

Keep in mind that a full tank of water can be very difficult. Then fill the system in the designated place and choose a stable box. After all, you don't want to risk the flood.

In order for the system to be refilled only once, approximately 5 liters per plant must be allowed. Each plant must have at least 20 cm^3 of space.

Note that these are obviously guidelines only and may vary by plant.

Also, consider purchasing a matte box; otherwise, algae will affect the system.

Pots and net substrate

As you already know, mesh pots are filled with substrate.

There is nothing serious to note about fish dishes. They should be stable enough to be reused.

As long as the substrate does not come into contact with the nutrient solution, any substrate can be used in a culture in deep water. Note the particle size. If the substrate falls into the nutrient solution, it can affect the pH.

We recommend hydroponics in deep water

- perlite,
- Rockwool,
- Vermiculite
- Spheres of expanded clay.

Of course, organic substrates such as coconut fibers are also suitable. However, the particles often enter the nutrient solution.

Floating platform / cover

Polystyrene is mainly used as a floating platform.

Polystyrene has the advantage of being readily available and has high flotation. Other materials often fail to keep the plants afloat at the end of the growth phase.

From an ecological point of view, we simply recommend using the cover. Although it is also made of plastic, it is much more resistant and less expensive.

Alternatively, a lacquered wooden board can be placed on the edges of the water tank.

The air pump and the air stone

As already mentioned, growing in shallow water can result in a lack of oxygen. To counter this, you need a small aquarium or pond air pump.

Typically, an air stone is included when purchasing an air pump. The pores should be as small as possible. The finer the pores, the more oxygen dissolves in the water.

The advantage of such aeration is evident in growth and yield. However, make sure that the air pump does not draw in too hot or too cold air. Otherwise, the extra air prevents growth.

Note: an air pump is not absolutely necessary. There are enough gardeners who can achieve a high yield in a deep water crop even without an air pump.

Troubleshooting

Although deepwater cultivation is a low maintenance hydroponic system, it can still cause unwanted problems.

If the roots turn brown or become soft, you should check

- Water temperature e
- the pH of the nutrient solution

If the plants grow slowly, you need to follow these instructions:

- EC value may be too low.
- Plants don't have enough light.
- Water is too cold (temperatures below 18 degrees should be avoided)
- Frequently Asked Questions About Deep Sea Culture

Which plants are suitable for growing in deep water?

Hydroponics in deep water was originally designed for tomatoes. Therefore, it is easily possible to plant large vegetables such as cucumbers and tomatoes.

An air pump is recommended because fruit plants generally require a lot of oxygen. Due to the high weight, it is not necessary to use a floating platform.

Only small plants such as salads or herbs are suitable for floating platforms.

A selection of suitable plants:

Plants very suitable for deep water cultivation: basil, celery, dill, fennel, cabbage, lettuce, nasturtium, chives, Swiss chard, sorrel, watercress, and brown mustard.

Not optimal, but possible: rocket, coriander, pepper,

Tomatoes, marigolds, mint, parsley, spinach, and strawberries.

HOW DO YOU BUILD A WATER TANK?

You don't want to use a plastic box, but you want to build a tank yourself? Then buy wooden slats and screw them together in a frame. Then you can extend the lining of the pond. Your water tank is ready!

How often is it necessary to replenish water and nutrients?

Whenever necessary. It is best to fill the system only once at the start. Of course, this assumes that the water tank is large enough. Water requirements vary depending on the plant.

For leafy vegetables, however, five liters per plant should be enough.

If it is still filled with the nutrient solution, it is necessary to recheck the pH and the EC value and, if necessary, modify them.

How big must the raft be?

Small raft plates can become too unstable in large plants. However, they are well suited for leafy greens.

Most rafts are 60cm * 120cm or 120cm * 240 cm. Adjust the size to the size of your system. There should be as little space as possible between the raft and the system; otherwise, too much light will enter the water reservoir.

Indoor or outdoor?

The location is entirely dependent on the lighting conditions and personal preferences.

If you have an indoor system, the plants should be illuminated with a plant lamp. Without enough light, the plants will not grow despite an efficient system.

If you prefer an outdoor system, you should be aware of the following points: Rain can wash out the nutrient solution and change the pH. The hydroponic system is also dependent on temperature fluctuations and sunlight.

Furthermore, the risk of pest infestation is significantly higher. If you prefer efficient growth and want to harvest your plants regularly, we recommend that you design your deepwater culture as an indoor system.

BUILD DEEP WATER CULTURE YOURSELF - TOOLS & EQUIPMENT

Fortunately, a deep water culture is quick and easy to build. Let's start with the tools and equipment. Hole drill

- The right tool :
- Drill / cordless drill
- Hole saw

The right equipment :

- Net pot
- Hydroponic fertilizer
- box
- Net pots
- Substrate
- Seedling in rockwool
- possibly plant lamps

INSTRUCTIONS: 5 STEPS TO DEEP WATER CULTURE (KRATKY METHOD)

Drill holes take the box and use the hole saw and drill to drill holes in the lid. The holes should be arranged so that each plant has at least 20 cm² of space.

The exact distance depends on the plant.

Fill in the nutrient solution.

After you have cleaned the system, you can fill in the nutrient solution. To do this, fill the box with water.

The water surface should be just below the net pots so that the roots reach the water, but the substrate in the net pot does not get wet.

Now mix in the hydroponic fertilizer and stir everything into a nutrient solution. Always pay attention to the pH and EC value of the nutrient solution.

Fill the net pots Next, put your seedling or young plant in the net pot, and fix the plant with a suitable substrate. The young plant is often raised in rock wool and coated with expanded clay.

It is best to inform yourself beforehand about the suitable hydroponic substrate.

Before you implement your seedling in the hydroponic system, roots at least 1-2 cm long should be visible.

Insert plants

While you were preparing the net pot, the pH of the nutrient solution settled. The best thing to do is to check it again and adjust it if necessary.

Now comes the long-awaited moment: placing the net pot and the plant in the deep water culture. Finally, check that the roots reach the nutrient solution; otherwise, your plant will die.

MAINTENANCE OF THE HYDROPONICS SYSTEM

If you want to promote the most efficient plant growth possible, place the deepwater culture under a strong plant lamp - especially in autumn or winter.

The system should also be easily accessible. This will make it easier for you to maintain your system.

Maintenance is necessary because, depending on the plant and growth stage, the nutrient solution has to be replaced or replenished in order to maintain the optimal growth conditions for your plant.

It is also important to check the root system and measure the pH at regular intervals.

Optimize the self-built deep water culture

Deep Water culture combines all the advantages of hydroponics, but there are even more efficient hydroponic systems, such as an NFT system.

Before you change your hydroponics system, you can optimize your self-built deep water culture.

An active deep water culture

Your hydroponic deep water culture has been in use for two weeks, but the plants are not growing properly. A look into the water reservoir is worthwhile at the latest. If the roots are brown, you should do the following.

Brown and rotten roots develop when the nutrient solution is under-saturated with oxygen - the major disadvantage of deep water culture.

In order to constantly supply the nutrient solution with sufficient oxygen, an air pump is often connected. The passive hydroponics system becomes an active hydroponics system.

Drill holes for the air hose and put the air stone under the roots. Optionally, you can operate the air pump with a timer. One air stone per plant is optimal, but not absolutely necessary.

Deep Water culture with a raft

Instead of a lid, you can also use a floating platform.

Drill suitable holes in, e.g., styrofoam, and place the raft on the nutrient solution. There should be as little space as possible around the edges to prevent the incidence of light.

What is an ebb and flow system?

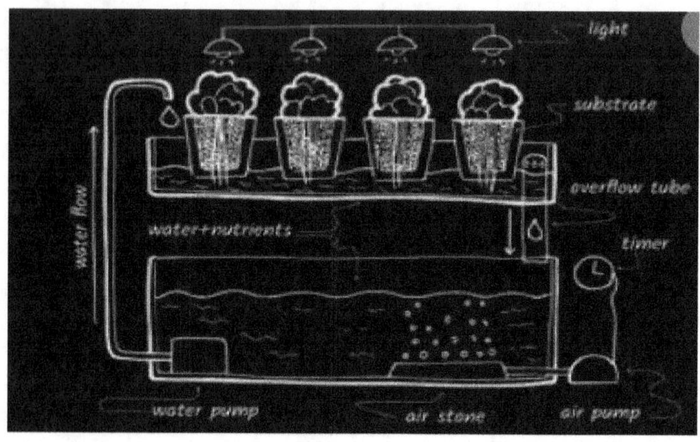

The ebb/flow/flood and drainage system is an active and circulating hydroponic system.

The system is active because a water pump pumps the nutrient solution to the roots of the plant. In addition, it circulates because the nutrient solution returns to the water tank after the flood, and the process starts again.

BENEFITS

- relatively inexpensive
- simple operation
- Low maintenance
- suitable for many plants
- low maintenance

Since the irrigation cycle is adapted to the needs of the plant, plants of different climates (dry or wet) can grow in an ebb and flow system.

DOWNSIDE

Risk of technical failure or power failure

fluctuating pH value due to nutrient deposits in the substrate

Since the system depends on the pump, factories can dry out in the event of a technical failure or power failure.

In addition, minerals are deposited in the substrate because it is repeatedly flooded with the nutrient solution. Deposits can affect the pH of the nutrient solution.

How does an ebb and flow system work?

Basically, an ebb and flow system always work the same way.

A water pump pumps water and nutrients to the roots. Then the water returns to the water tank. You can use a timer to set the flood frequency of the plant container.

So far, so good - but how does the nutrient solution work without causing floods? Since this has not yet been definitively clarified, two options are explained below.

Ebb and flow system with overflow

In this variant, the nutrient solution passes through a simple tube.

To reach the desired water level in the system container, the pumping capacity must be greater than the water flowing through the drain.

To avoid flooding, the water pump pumps up to fill the planter. The filling time is measured in advance, and the timer is adjusted accordingly.

Ebb and flow system with overflow

This variation of an ebb and flow system is advantageous as only a single pump, and a simple overflow (single pipe) are needed.

However, flooding can occur even if the overflow is blocked by the substrate. A second higher overflow can remedy this.

Ebb and flow system with a bell siphon

Graphic bell trap

An ebb and flow system can also be drained with a bell siphon. A bell siphon uses physics to empty the plant container safely and reliably.

If the water pressure in the system container reaches a critical level, the siphon empties the system container. More water should drain than the pump can pump into the system container simultaneously.

Ventilation and oxygen

It is important to always make sure that there is enough oxygen in the nutrient solution.

When the nutrient solution falls back into the water tank in abundance or with the siphon, the oxygen content in the water increases.

Otherwise, an air pump can enrich the water tank with oxygen.

MATERIAL AND EQUIPMENT

- a water tank,
- a plant pot,
- a water pump,
- an overflow/bell siphon,
- a timer,
- an appropriate substrate
- and possibly net pots.

The water tank

To prevent algae growth, the water tank must be opaque.

The volume of the water tank varies depending on whether you use mesh pots or fill the entire substrate of the plant with the substrate.

If mesh pots are used, the volume of the water tank should be at least 20% greater than the volume of the plant container.

In the latter case, the volume of the plant container and the water tank can be the same because the substrate in the plant container moves enough water.

The vase

The size of the plant container depends on the size and number of plants. Therefore, only one guideline can be provided.

For most plants, the plant container should be 30 cm deep. Likewise, many plants need 30 cm in width. When buying, keep in mind that the substrate and nutrient solution is heavy. Therefore, the plant container must be very robust. It should also be opaque.

Water pump

It is not necessary to quickly flood the planter.

Therefore, inexpensive water pumps with low pumping capacity are sufficient. For example, with a 300-liter planter, a water pump with a capacity of 100 liters per hour is sufficient.

Siphon and bell overflow

When the water pressure in the system container reaches a fixed level (about five centimeters below the surface of the substrate), the siphon begins to empty the system container. In this case, more water must flow out than what is pumped.

In the event of an overflow, however, it must be able to drain less water than what can be pumped simultaneously. Pay attention to the respective diameter in both variants. Likewise, in both cases, the nutrient solution must fall as deep as possible into the water tank to increase the oxygen content.

The timer

The timer is only required for a flow and reflux system in combination with an overflow.

As soon as the system is installed, the time taken by the water pump to fill the plant container (including plants, substrate, and overflow) with the nutrient solution is measured.

The service life of the pump and the watering time are adjusted accordingly.

The frequency of watering the plant pot depends entirely on the substrate and the needs of the plant. The following applies: prove relates to the study. As a rule, the plant container should be flooded at least twice a day.

The substrate

The selection of the substrate for an ebb and flow system depends on the needs of the plant.

Expanded clay spheres as a substrate for hydroponics

Expanded clay spheres

If the plant "likes water," substrates that store water such as vermiculite, coconut fiber, or rock wool should be used.

Unlike this, substrates with good drainages, such as perlite or expanded clay, should be used for plants that are preferably "dry lovers."

Different substrates can be mixed to improve the properties.

Plants for an ebb and flow system

You are spoiled for choice. Due to individual irrigation, almost all plants are suitable for a hydroponic ebb and flow system.

Plants in dry climates can also thrive with the right substrate.

Here is a small selection of suitable plants:

- Salad (all types)
- Herbs (eg, Basil, coriander, thyme, mint and dill)
- strawberries
- Water chestnut
- Asian vegetables
- Peppers and peppers

- Radishes, carrots, and beets.
- Tomatoes, cucumbers, broccoli, and cabbage

Some gardeners even use an ebb and flow system for germination and seed selection.

Maintenance and upkeep

The substrate should be removed from the system at least every six to twelve months and thoroughly rinsed with clean water.

If the pH of the nutrient solution fluctuates too much, the substrate should also be cleaned and the minerals removed. In the event of a pest infestation, the substrate and the system must be sterilized with detergent.

Conclusion

The ebb and flow system is one of the best known hydroponic systems and is very efficient. If handled properly, very high yields are possible.

The system impresses with its controlled supply of water and nutrients and therefore allows the cultivation of many types of vegetables and herbs.

However, the irrigation cycle requires certain skills. Some experience is an advantage so that the power of the pump, the drainage, and the timer is adapted to the needs of the system.

However, beginners can, of course also try a small ebb and flow system. If the system is used as an indoor garden, fresh herbs and delicious vegetables can be harvested all year round.

Nutrient Film Technique (NFT) system

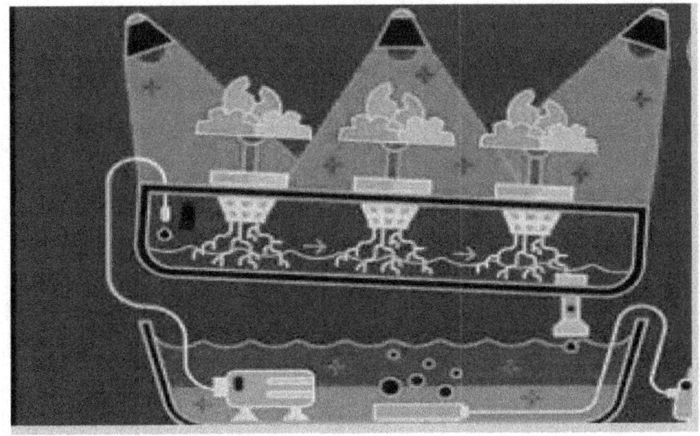

The Nutrient Film Technique (NFT) system was invented in 1979 by the Englishman Allen Cooper. This culture system used by horticulture professionals does not require a substrate but requires a pathogen-free nutrient solution.

The decoding of the acronym Nutrient Film Technique (NFT) shows us the operating principle of this system.

Operation

Nutrient Film Technique, or technique on nutritious film in French,

The plants are arranged with their clods of substrates (rock wool, or other) on gutters or culture trays slightly inclined (1 to 2%). An opaque tarpaulin provides the necessary darkness for the roots. The nutrient solution is injected into the upper part and flows to the lower part where it is collected and then reinjected.

The nutritive fluid circulates on the trays in the form of a thin film which comes into contact with the roots. These develop on a root carpet (non-woven fiber canvas). The nutrient solution is oxygenated by its movement in the gutters and by the large surface area for the exchange of liquid with air.

Indeed, imagine a volume of nutrient solution circulating on the gutters: (1 Liter, for example.)

With a thickness of 1 cm (this is exaggerated), this nutritious "flow" representing an area of contact with air of 0.1 m^2

This same liter of nutritive solution which flows in the form of a film of 1 mm (0.1 cm) has a surface of contact with the air of 1 m^2,

The thinner the volume, the larger the air exchange surface, and the efficient ventilation.

Benefits

The Nutrient Film Technique (NFT) system has many advantages that make it a performing system:

- NFT systems have a limited height, which makes it possible to optimize the height space and avoid burning the top of the plants under the action of the heat of the horticultural bulbs.
- We forget the substrate, which is not negligible. The 75 mm stone wool cubes are sufficient. Those of 100 mm will ensure better stability for the plants.

- Cleaning/disinfection is very fast because a few parts make up this system.
- Accessibility to plants is good since the gutters are generally raised. This allows working at breast height.
- The main advantage lies in the low volumes of the nutritive solution necessary to carry out a culture. This system "recycles" the nutrient solution, so we limit the consumption of inputs (water, fertilizers, additives).
- It is also difficult to over-water in NFT, which makes it an excellent system for beginners.
- It is also possible to install a heating device in the tank and quickly reach a desired temperature at the roots. Growth or yield will be increased (an advantage which also results from the limited volume of nutrient solution)

However, the main advantages of NFT lead to the disadvantages of this system

Disadvantages

The absence of substrates (which would constitute a water and mineral reserve) requires daily monitoring of the functioning of the system (homogeneous flow of the nutrient solution) and a rapid reaction in the event of a pump failure.

In this regard, it is better to have a spare pump. Forewarned is forearmed!

The cultivator's nightmare on NFT is the prolonged blackout, especially for horticulturalists with extensive systems (above ground). The only solution for them is to equip themselves with a generator.

If the situation arises, plant transpiration should be kept to a minimum; this goes through:

- the bulbs go out if they work,
- the decrease in air temperature. (Maintain a minimum acceptable temperature for cultivated plants.),
- an increase in humidity (air humidity),
- misting plants with water.

With modest Nutrient Film Technical (NFT) systems, power outages are easier to manage. It is possible to water the root ball of each plant individually with a watering can to avoid water stress while waiting for the electricity fairy.

Another drawback of this system is observed when the temperatures are high in the culture space. The tank is filled with a small volume of nutrient solution (this was an advantage because less water and fertilizer are consumed), the thermal inertia * is low, and the heating of the nutrient solution is significant. (* thermal inertia is the ability of a material, the nutrient solution in our case, to resist temperature variations). Clearly, the temperature of the nutritious soup can rise suddenly and reach a level that can be dangerously high for the plants.

Indeed, the higher the temperature of a liquid, the less it can contain oxygen, an essential element for the functioning of the roots. This is why this system is rarely encountered in southern or tropical countries.

Finally, the major drawback specific to closed-loop systems is the spread of plant diseases/pathogens throughout the crop.

Substrate

The main advantage of growing on a nutritious film is that it does not require a substrate, except for a cube of rock wool, which ensures the maintenance of the plant.

Irrigation

As the acronym NFT indicates, the supply of water and minerals is carried out thanks to a film of the nutritive solution, a light trickle of water which will flow continuously on the roots. An excessive supply of nutrient solution will create a lack of oxygen in the roots and will make the plants susceptible to root diseases (pythium, phytophthora)

This system operates in a closed circuit. In order to ensure the mineral nutrition of plants, the nutrient solution, pH, and electroconductivity (EC) should be checked frequently and readjusted as necessary.

Build your own NFT system (equipment)

Building your own NFT system yourself is easier than it looks. Don't be put off by the pipe construction, but instead enjoy the nice feeling of having created something with your own hands. If you don't have the time or don't feel like it, you can also buy an NFT system.

For those who want to build an NFT system themselves, pay attention now! In the following, you will find out what you need for an NFT system and what you have to pay attention to.

- Water reservoir
- water pump
- Tube
- Net pots
- Substrate
- Hoses or pipes
- Water reservoir

A stable water reservoir is essential for a solid NFT system. It stores the nutrient solution and is placed under the tubes.

Most often, a plastic box is used as a reservoir. This should be stable, and it's plastic suitable for cultivation. This is particularly important if the box is exposed to direct sunlight.

NFT tubes

The NFT system is the only hydroponic system in which the plants do not grow in a box, but in tubes.

Simple PVC pipes are suitable for the pipes. However, these have the disadvantage that the water flows down in a channel. The risk of root constipation and uneven supply is increased.

Therefore, pipes with a flat bottom should preferably be used. However, these are usually expensive and difficult to get.

If you use simple PVC pipes, it is particularly important to set the inclination correctly so that the nutrient solution does not pass the roots too quickly or too slowly. Otherwise, growth problems are inevitable.

Another important aspect is the length. The first plants in a gutter receive more nutrients than plants at the end of a gutter.

The channel length should be limited to 10-15 meters so that there are no excessive differences in plant growth. If you don't want to do without longer channels, you should set up a new nutrient inflow at similar intervals.

Water pump

For a small NFT system with approx. 10 plants, a simple pond water pump from the hardware store, is sufficient. The pumping capacity is usually sufficient for a water reservoir of 100 liters.

Hoses, pipes & tees

So that each plant container (tube) can be supplied with a nutrient solution, you need T-pieces that divide and pass on the water. Depending on the system structure, the nutrient solution can be transported to the plants via hoses or pipes.

It is very important that the transport routes are opaque; otherwise, algae can form. Removing algae is complex and not something you want to spend your time with.

Flow rate

The inclination of the channel should be 1:16. In plain language, this means that a 16 cm long channel should have a height difference of 1 cm. So an incline of about 6 percent or about 4 degrees. With a lower gradient, there is a higher risk of traffic jams.

Interview

Maintenance consists of a Nutrient Film Technical System (NFT), as for other hydroponic devices, to run the Nutrient Film Technical System (NFT) with a disinfectant solution (Hydrogen peroxide, Bleach). , which will ensure the cleanliness of the gutters/culture tray and the distribution circuit. Do not forget to. Clean the pump.

Drip system and drip irrigation

Have you ever seen a hose in the flower bed from which small drops of water run out? If so, then you got to know drip irrigation - a very efficient irrigation technique.

Drip irrigation was developed by Simcha Blass. The engineer and inventor presented his first time-controlled drip irrigation to the public around 1950 - with great success.

In the following decades, drip irrigation was combined with hydroponics. The drip system of hydroponics was born. For the first time, it was now possible to supply several plants individually with the same nutrient solution.

WHAT IS A DRIP SYSTEM?

A drip system is an active hydroponic system and supplies plants with the nutrient solution by means of drip irrigation. With drip irrigation, water flows through a hose with small holes from which the water reaches the roots.

Layout and function

There are now many different variations of a hydroponic drip system. However, the mode of operation is the same for everyone.

The (basic) drip system of hydroponics supplies the plants with drip irrigation. For this purpose, a water pump pumps the nutrient solution out of the water reservoir through the hose construction. In most cases, drip nozzles are connected to the hose, from which the nutrient solution drips out.

Excess nutrient solution drips from the net pots into the collecting container and runs back into the water reservoir.

Properties

With proper handling, the plants thrive splendidly and deliver high yields. But why is that, and what makes the drip system so special? There are 3 reasons for this:

Optimal control over water and nutrient supply

The water and nutrient supply can be perfectly regulated and adapted to the plants. You either change the water pressure or regulate the drip nozzles. Therefore, the drip system is suitable for many different types of plants.

Individual care

The drip nozzles allow individual irrigation. The irrigation intensity can be set at the nozzle. Different plant species in different growth stages can, therefore, be individually supplied with the same nutrient solution.

Scalability

A drip system can be expanded quickly and easily - as long as the pumping capacity is sufficient. Simply expand the hose and add more plants. For this reason, the drip system can often be found in commercial hydroponics.

Overview of the properties of a drip system:

- active   Yes
- passive No
- Circulating   Yes No
- Air pump   optional
- water pump   Yes

- Crop yield   high
- Nutrient supply   high
- Oxygen supply   high

Equipment for a drip system

A drip system is easy to build, even if it doesn't seem that way at first glance. For a (basic) drip system you need:

Water reservoir: The container should be closed and opaque to prevent algae from growing. The nutrient solution is stored in the water reservoir. This can be replenished if necessary.

Mesh pots: With a drip system, you need mesh pots for the plants. However, you do not need mesh pots if the collecting container is completely filled with substrate.

Water pump: For a small drip system, pumping between 200 and 400 liters per minute is sufficient.

Drip nozzles: One drip nozzle per plant is completely sufficient.

Hoses: The drip nozzles are connected with thin hoses.

Timer: A timer needs you only if you plant only occasionally want to irrigate. With continuous irrigation, the timer is not applicable.

Substrate: The substrate plays an important role. The irrigation intensity depends on the properties of the substrate. If the substrate stores a lot of water, for example, a low irrigation intensity is required.

Suitable plants and substrates for a drip system

Due to the control of the individual supply intensity with water and nutrients, many plants are particularly suitable for a drip system in hydroponics. A drip system is primarily intended for larger plants. Above all, this includes fruit plants.

Melon in a hydroponic drip system

Plants that grow in a drip system:

- tomatoes
- Cucumbers
- salad
- zucchini
- Melons
- Pumpkins
- Peas
- Strawberries

There are many more plants that grow in hydroponics.

When choosing the substrate, the requirements of the respective plant must be observed. Moisture-loving plants prefer substrates with a high water storage capacity—for example, coconut fibers, vermiculite, or rock wool. In contrast, substrates with a low water storage capacity are expanded clay balls, pearlite, or gravel.

MAINTENANCE AND CARE

As soon as the drip system is installed correctly, the effort remains manageable. The most common problem is the clogging of the drip nozzles. Over time, salts from the nutrient solution are deposited. To avoid the problem, the entire system should be flushed after a harvest cycle.

As with other hydroponic systems, regular control of the nutrient solution is important. The pH should be checked weekly. If there is a fresh nutrient solution in the system, the pH value should be observed right at the beginning.

In addition to the pH value, the EC value and the temperature must also be observed. Both values should be in the ideal range of the plant.

Summary

The drip system is a very efficient and simple hydroponic system. The system is also scalable, supplies plants individually, and is suitable for a wide variety of plant types. The great variety of suitable plants make the system so special.

Advantages:

- Precise control over water and nutrient supply
- Affordable purchase price
- Low maintenance
- Scalable system
- Very efficient

Disadvantages:

- Designing the system and adjusting the irrigation intensity requires some experience.
- Wasted nutrient solution in a non-circulating drip system.
- Increased maintenance requirements for a circulating system.

Substrates and environment

The use of a growing medium necessarily has an impact on our environment.

The manufacture of a substrate requires more or less energy for the extraction of raw materials, their transformation (often by heating), the packaging of the substrate, and finally, its transport to the place of sale and then to the place of use. And this energy, which is used to move backhoes, trucks, comes from fairly polluting fossil fuels (CO_2, NO_x, SO_x,).

There are other factors impacting the quality of water, air. There is no ecological substrate but only supports of cultures whose manufacture (or elimination) more or less impacts the environment.

The future of hydroponics rests on cropping systems that do NOT use a growing medium.

Aeroponic or aquaponic systems make it possible to limit the consumption of substrate and in addition to reducing the time for setting up a culture. (no substrates to disinfect/replace for example)

Agricultural or industrial by-products can constitute horticultural substrates more or less respectful of the environment due to their revalorization (instead of "classic" substrate): cereal straw, flax, sawdust, and bark of wood, grape marc.

These substrates tend to settle gradually, thus reducing the aeration of the roots. In addition, these products are not really chemically stable (despite their composting), and a release of phytotoxic substances can irreparably damage a culture (Phytotoxic: from the Greek Python, "vegetable and toxic" poison "). These substrates are to be tested on a batch of sample plants.

Here is a summary table of the characteristics of hydroponic substrates:

	Coconut fibers	Rockwool	Vermiculite	Perlite	Expanded clay	pozzolan
Physical characteristics						
Bulk density (kg / m³)	40 to 90	50 to 70	80 to 130	80 to 120	400 to 800	500 to 1200
Porosity	95%	90 to 95	95%	90 to 95%	70 to 85	> to 70%
Water availability	15 to 35%	70	5 to 10%	5 to 10%	1 to 10%	5 to 10%
Chemical characteristics						
Cation exchange capacity (meq / 100g)	25 to 90	nothing	50 to 100	nothing	nothing	nothing
Electric conductivity (mS.cm-1)	0.3 or more depending on origin	nothing	0.04 to 0.05	0.02	0.1 to 0.2 after leaching	0.001 to 0.003
pH (water)	5 to 6.5	7 to 9	6 to 8	About 7	7	6 to 7

Rock wool, the ideal hydroponic substrate.

ROCK WOOL MANUFACTURING

Rock wool is a substrate obtained only by industrial processes.

The raw material is a mixture of basalt rock (diabase for service geologists), limestone, and coke (nm: product obtained from the carbonization or distillation of coal). This mixture is brought to 1500 ° C. Then fibers are extracted from this paste, are then bonded together and coated with a hydrophilic wetting agent. This last step is specific to horticultural rock wool (Not the one used for thermal insulation of buildings) These fibers are organized to allow colonization of the substrate by the roots and facilitate the removal of water and minerals. The substrate is then packaged in the form of flakes, corks, cubes, or bread.

The plugs are small pieces of rock wool suitable for sowing and cutting. There are different sizes: 25, 36 or 40mm side)

The cubes are larger (75 to 100mm side) and are used for the start of plant growth. They are used alone in NFT systems.

Rockwool bread is reserved for plants carrying out their entire growing cycle. They have a dimension of 100 x 15 x 7.50mm.

USE

The installation of rockwool cubes on the bread is simple. The protective cover of the bread is torn (often made of white polyethylene) in a cross pattern, and the cubes are simply placed on the bread. The plastic will be folded over the cubes to avoid the development of algae.

Rock wool is suitable for hydroponic systems by percolation. Indeed, this technique allows precise contributions of the nutritive solution.

There is gutters/planter (Aquatray - Librabac) specially dimensioned to receive the rockwool bread and allowing to create its custom hydroponic device: pipes, elbows of the tees, some drippers, a tank of nutritive solution and c' left for the horticultural adventure.

Some growers use this substrate on tide tables with good results. Since this substrate has excellent water retention, it is preferable not to "drown" it, especially if the cultivated species are sensitive to stagnation of water at the roots.

Rock wool is a substrate with a basic pH (7.5 to 9) too high for plants grown above ground. This phenomenon is caused among other things by the release of Calcium and magnesium. It is for this reason that the pH continues to rise at the start of the culture, then stabilizes.

It is, therefore, preferable to soak/immerse the rock wool in water with a pH of 5.0 to 5.5 for 24 hours before cultivation.

Thus, the rock wool will have a satisfactory pH and will be really inert.

INSTALLATION OF ROCKWOOL.

Rock wool is an "agglomerate" of artificial fibers. The dry fibers are thin and light enough to be inhaled through a man's respiratory tract and to lodge in the lungs. All precautions must be taken during installation: mask, gloves, long sleeves, and protective glasses, wool rock is irritating.

This problem no longer arises once the rock wool is in the presence of water. The hydrophilic wetting agent makes the fibers increase the water content of the substrate, making the fibers heavier, less transportable by air currents.

This can be done easily with cubes (directly in a bucket) but becomes more complicated for loaves of 100 x 15 x 7.5 cm. We can then buffer the substrate directly in the culture device, by making it "turn empty" in an open circuit preferably (closed if the volume of the tank is large):

For this, it is necessary to install the loaves in the space provided for this purpose, fill the tank with water with rectified pH, set up the drippers, and switch on the distribution pump. The substrate must be perfectly saturated with water.

Rock wool bread has a precise direction of installation (An arrow on the polyethylene cover indicates the direction to respect. (This side up!) Finally, the drainage holes, allowing to evacuate the excess nutrient solution, are already present on some bread. Otherwise, have fun making a few lacerations on the protective cover on the underside.

Regarding its properties (physical and chemical), rock wool is certainly the lightest substrate and the one that retains the most water! It's a real sponge, which makes irrigation quite technical, at least at the start.

Rule no 1: Plants that grow in support like Rockwool require frequent watering but in small quantities. Never saturate/drown the rock wool; otherwise the roots will suffocate! (Water takes up all the space available in the "voids" of the substrate, air, and oxygen, in particular, is absent/limited, hence suffocation)

Rule no 2: Add the excess nutrient solution so as to obtain 15 to 20% drainage. This is to avoid accumulations of salts in the substrate.

Rule no 3: Always drain drainage effluents from rock wool. In this case, the pH of the substrate will skyrocket.

Rule no 4: The pH and electroconductivity (EC) testers are absolutely necessary when growing on rockwool. Indeed, this substrate is completely inert, has no buffering capacity (ability to oppose variations in pH, EC). The slightest error in the formulation of the nutrient solution is immediately seen in the culture. Therefore, it is a substrate that is not suitable for beginners but rather for people with experience of hydroponic crops.

Benefits

- Thanks to its properties, rock wool is close to the ideal substrate for hydroponic crops:
- It is chemically inert, does not modify the nutritive solution by the release of minerals (in practice is after soaking in water at pH rectified)
- It does not degrade, retains its mechanical strength, which ensures maintenance of physical properties (air, water content)
- It does not contain pathogens (fungi, viruses, bacteria), phytotoxic products (tannins, resins), weed seeds ("weeds").

Disadvantages

However, as we have seen in its manufacture, this substrate requires a large amount of energy, which does not make it a particularly "ecological" substrate. Especially since the disposal of rock wool is problematic:

- Some producers eliminate bread by shredding them into pieces and incorporating them into the fields (in lowland).
- Amateur gardeners will also shred it and incorporate it into the soil for potted plants (watering spacing).
- Rock wool will disintegrate over time, but the fibers will still be present in the soil.
- This substrate is never reused after a culture, even if it is technically possible (after removing the maximum of the roots and eliminating the excess of salts). Professionals use steam to disinfect their substrates.

Rock wool sometimes becomes covered with green algae. Indeed, the substrate is particularly humid, rich in nutrients, and the temperature high. A little light is enough to have a real explosion of algae. These proliferate and can compete with the plant for nutrients and water. But it is mainly because algae can become a breeding ground for the development of pathogens. There are products allowing to control of these algae. To avoid this development of algae, it is better to hide the substrate from the light rays (this is why the bread is bagged).

PERLITE AS A SUBSTRATE FOR HYDROPONICS.

Perlite manufacturing

Perlite is in the form of white grains, very light but very brittle.

The perlite comes from rapid heating of silica sand to 1000 ° C, which causes the water vaporization of the grains of sand and their sudden expansions (x 4 to x 20), much like the grain of corn, which becomes popcorn…

The shape of this substrate (very light flakes) allows rapid implementation in the culture system (essentially by drip percolation). The wearing of a protective mask is strongly advised (beware of silicosis!) Because there is always a release of dust likely to be lodged in the lungs. Spraying water on the substrate before handling will limit the escape of dust.

Advantage of Perlite

- Perlite has very interesting chemical properties for growers in hydroponics.
- A pH between 6.8 and 7.2, a zero buffering capacity allowing precise control of fertilization (but beware of dosing errors…).
- But it is mainly thanks to its high porosity that perlite is used above ground. (This is also why perlite is used as a thermal insulator).
- Perlite is used "pure" in tubs or gutters with drip irrigation.

Disadvantages

But, as much as the physical characteristics of the perlite is good (high porosity, low density), as much these mechanical characteristics leave something to be desired: the perlite is easily brittle and settles as the mass of the plant increases.

The total porosity of the perlite decreases at the same time as the compaction increases, and the porous grains of perlite become fine white powder.

Common use

To cope with this low mechanical resistance of perlite, it is often associated with other substrates (coconut fibers, peat), where it provides ventilation for the nutrient solution and the root system. In this case, the perlite should not represent more than 30% of the mixture. under penalty of creating heterogeneous zones in the substrate. ("Pockets" of perlite or the roots may dehydrate quickly.)

Perlite is used in seed trays, where it was mixed with vermiculite. :(50-50)

Perlite is a substrate that is easily eliminated in the garden in the ground, or mixed with a potting soil that does not contain it. For potted plants. It will disintegrate over time into dust without leaving traces.

GARDEX, THE SUBSTRATE FOR BEGINNERS IN HYDROPONICS

Composition

Gardex is a substrate made from a mixture of mineral wool fibers (such as rock wool), perlite, vermiculite. . This substrate is free of pathogens (by their manufacturing methods, the ingredients entering the composition of Gardex are heated to temperatures of at least 1000 ° C)

Vermiculite, perlite, rock wool, hydro-retensor.

Density: dry 0.16 - saturated with water 0.7

Total porosity: dry 93% saturated with water 30 to 33% (volume)
Water retention: 58 to 61% (volume)
Water available 45 to 49% (volume)
ph 6.8 to 7.2

USE

Originally intended for landscapers to be used as a substrate for a planter or a hanging garden that is difficult to access, "Gardex" has been slightly diverted from its main use to be used as a cutting medium or even as a substrate for plants with very few roots. .

Gardex is very similar in its use to sphagnum.

Irrigation should be carried out with a complete soluble fertilizer. (hydroponic fertilizer) even if a slow-release fertilizer (for 6 months) is already integrated into the substrate. (Nutrient reserve)

To find out if the nutrient intakes are sufficient or in excess, measure the EC (electroconductive) of the nutrient solution and compare with the EC of the drainage water. (If the drainage EC is higher than the nutrient solution EC, the fertilization must be lowered)

Benefits

The green space services which use it particularly appreciate this substrate: a hydro retentor (crosslinked polyacrylamides to be exact) is added to reduce the frequency of watering.

- Maximum ventilation.
- Increased water retention.
- Clean and light.

- Neutral pH, ideal for many plants.
- Accelerated growth.
- Brighter foliage.
- Homogeneous distribution of the root system.
- More abundant and more colorful flowering.
- Very significant reduction in the frequency of watering and easy rehydration.
- constant volume (no compaction)
- Sterile (treated at more than 1000 °, no diseases.)

Gardex constitutes a substrate of choice for the person taking their first steps in the world of hydroponics. The water and nutrient reserves of the mixture allow to overcome small mistakes of beginners.

EXPANDED CLAY BALLS

Expanded clay beads have different advantages that make them a popular substrate for home gardeners. Their rounded shapes, their colors, their particularly aesthetic appearance for a substrate mean that they are encountered in plant containers in shopping centers, medical offices, at your mothers-in-law's, etc.

The expanded clay beads constitute the reference substrate for gardeners using the "hydroculture" technique, passive hydroponics.

As its name suggests, this substrate is made of clay, materials that are found abundantly in the countries of northern Europe (Denmark, Germany) where the beads were created.

There are different grain sizes: 1/4, 4/8, 8/16, or 10 / 20mm.

Manufacturing of expanded clay beads

The production of this substrate follows the following stages:

- After extraction from the quarries, the clay is kneaded to homogenize it. The presence of water makes it more plastic and, therefore, easier to work with.
- Then we form the clay balls,
- Finally, after brief cooking at 1100 ° C, the clay pellets lost all their water and underwent a start of vitrification on their surface.

Benefits of transforming clay into expanded clay beads.

This cooking has several consequences on clay:

- Like all cooking of this material (see pottery), the clay solidifies (loss of its plasticity). The result is a very stable substrate, which retains its physical properties: they do not settle.
- The brutal vaporization of the clay water creates a large internal porosity but closed. It is the myriad of bubbles (which we observe inside the broken beads) that make this substrate so light.
- The vitrification of the surface of the clay beads makes them completely inert from a chemical point of view: they neither retain nor release nutrients.

This makes it a substrate of choice for hydroponic crops.

However, like all substrates, the expanded clay beads retain some ions (Calcium and Potassium) as the culture lasts.

As we saw previously, the expanded clay beads have a closed internal porosity. This means that the air bubbles inside the balls are not in communication with the outside. The practical and hydroponic consequence is that fluids (air or nutrient solution) cannot enter these beads. This is why this substrate does not retain water.

It is for this reason that in hydroponic devices using this growing medium, irrigation cycles are very frequent. Irrigation can, therefore, be continuous, but slightly limiting the flow of the drippers (or the pump)

As the clay balls are very draining, it is almost impossible to water them excessively. Finally, a layer of expanded clay at the bottom of a pot ensures the drainage of any substrate

But how does this substrate participate in the aeration of the nutrient solution?

Take the case of a percolation system with our expanded clay beads as a culture medium. The drop of nutrient solution (which has just come out of the drippers) spreads over the ball, covering its surface, (it changes color taking a darker shade), thus creating a thin film of nutrient solution which flows on the balls below thanks to gravity.

It is the large contact surface between the film of water and nutrients and the air that aerates the nutrient solution. The roughness of the clay balls increases the surface of contact with the air. Aeration is based on the same principle as the hydroponic system by NFT.

Expanded clay balls easily recreate the same conditions of humidity and aeration as in soil: The upper part is very airy while the layer of expanded clay located at the base is saturated with moisture.

Tips and tricks

Finally, the expanded clay beads must be rinsed thoroughly with water before first use. The goal is to remove the dust from the beads that have been created by friction between them. This dust has an impact on plant nutrition. Indeed, it releases chemical elements and increases the salinity (Electroconductivity; EC) of the nutritive solution.

COCONUT FIBER SUBSTRATE: COIR

Coconut fibers obviously come from coconut palms (Cocos nucifera.). It is a palm tree growing on the edge of the beach and which gives the famous coconuts. There are many uses: food (the pulp is edible) industrial (oil mills) and cosmetics.

Fibers are also used for making ropes, fabrics, carpets, etc. and wood for construction. For the anecdote, we also make etchings on coconuts!

In short, with all these uses, the coconut palm is a bit of a pig in the plant world! But back to our coconut fibers, which will provide the substrate.

They come from the "shell" (more precisely, the mesocarp, it is the stringy substance contained between the epidermis and the internal film) of the coconut.

The fibers undergo retting (prolonged soaking in freshwater) which allows the fibers to be separated from one another and to eliminate the salt (sodium chloride: sea salt from the spray).

In high concentrations, chlorine, but especially sodium are toxic to plants. (Except for halophilic plants like samphire!)

After composting, which stabilizes the chemical and physical characteristics of the future substrate, the fibers are calibrated and then bagged. Some manufacturers "seed" coconut fiber with beneficial microorganisms of the genus Trichoderma. These fungi initially prevent the establishment of a pathogenic fungus and then limit its spread over the entire crop.

Most of the production is carried out in India and Sri Lanka. The coconut fibers reach us by boat; they are packaged in big bags, 50l bags, loaves of 100 x 15 x 7.5 cm, or in compressed bricks.

USE OF COCONUT FIBERS

Coconut fiber is a substrate that can be used pure or mixed (10 to 20% perlite to improve drainage). It can be used in devices by percolation (drip) in sub-irrigation (with a layer of expanded clay at the base of the pot to improve drainage).

This substrate having a CEC (Def: see end of the comparison table of the characteristics of substrates), it has the capacity to store ions. The fibers can become increasingly "salty", accumulating large amounts of nutrients. (may become toxic). We must pay attention to this phenomenon in hydroponics; To avoid this build-up, always sprinkle the coconut fibers excessively. If, despite everything, the ions accumulate, it is necessary to rinse the coconut fibers with a very dilute nutritive solution.

There are also different solutions that remove excess salts (see rinse aid still allowed) But the best precaution is to never overdose fertilizers, especially in coconuts.

CHARACTERISTICS OF COCONUT FIBERS:

The coconut fibers have high water retention and capillary power which allows to space the irrigation cycles. (The coconut fibers must never be drowned)

The strong points of coconut fibers lie in the great stability of its structure (the lifespan of the fibers is 10 years). In addition, these fibers ensure good distribution of air and water in the substrate, especially after the addition of water.

Finally, the elimination of coconut fibers at the end of life does not pose problems like rock wool. The coconut can be reused advantageously in the vegetable garden as an organic amendment. (it will improve the soil structure)

The weak point mainly concerns the variability of the chemical characteristics as a function of supply. The presence of sea salts, rapid degradation of the fibers shows that certain stages of manufacturing have been botched (ex: rinsing, composting)

Green plants and light:

Photosynthesis is a photochemical process where light (solar) energy is converted into chemical energy, usable by the plant.

This energy is used for the extraction and transformation of mineral substances into organic substances. Photosynthesis is, therefore, the process underlying the production of plant matter.

The balance of photosynthesis is as follows:

$6\ CO_2 + 12\ H_2O + (Light\ energy) => C_6H_{12}O_6 + 6\ H_2O + O_2$ ***

The factory in which these transformations take place is the leaf. The beginning of the production chain begins in the chloroplast. It is at the heart of this workshop (on the surface of the thylakoids) that the reaction begins. Light rays excite chlorophyll, and the magic of photosynthesis can take place.

We could explain precisely the mechanism of photosynthesis (Photolysis of water, Calvin cycle), but the goal is to understand thanks to the photosynthesis balance that light is, with water and CO2, at the basis of life vegetable. (and therefore, animal.). Light is, therefore, the most important environmental factor for plants. (also the temperature, the CO2 level)

Plants have very different light needs. They vary according to several factors:

- The type of plants: (shade or light)
- From the growth stage (sowing, vegetative growth, maturation)
- External factors (temperature, CO2 content in the air, humidity, availability of water at the roots)

Light requirements: light intensity

Difference between cinephile and heliophilous plants

Not all plants have the same needs in terms of light intensity.

Certainly, plants such as ferns, cocoa, coffee require little light. They are called cinephiles.

Plants in the open field, or heliophilous, (cereals, market garden plants), meanwhile require a higher light intensity.

The difference between these plants lies in the compensation point for light, where photosynthesis (production of sugars) and respiration (transformation of sugars into energy) are in equilibrium. To simplify, the light requirement of a plant depends on the balance between the degradation of sugars resulting from photosynthesis and their manufacture.

The energy yields are, therefore, not the same according to these two types of plants. (energy used to produce the same plant mass). Conversion to chemical energy is better in shade plants (scrapes) than in sun plants (sunflowers)

Plants grown in hydroponics are mostly light plants and therefore require intense lighting. It is for this reason that greenhouses for the production of vegetables (tomatoes, cucumbers) are designed to allow good illumination of crops (Covering materials have good light transmission, tall structures limit shaded areas).

The high light intensity induces an increase in photosynthetic intensity, provided that other environmental factors are favorable (air temperature, CO_2 content in the air, etc.)

This increase in photosynthetic activity results in an increase in yield for the horticulturalists.

Gardeners with hydroponic systems under horticultural shelters (greenhouses, tunnels) benefit from the most intense light source: the sun.

This "big lamp" suspended in the middle of our solar system provides us with nearly 100,000 lux at the Zenith! In overcast skies, this intensity drops to 25,000 lux.

For comparison, the light intensity is from 1,000 to 10,000 lux in horticultural production greenhouses, from 3,000 to 10,000 on a surgical operating table (even if it is often dark ...) 800 lux in laboratories, 400 lux in classrooms, 50 lux in elevators and 0.2 lux per full moon night.

However, sometimes the lighting under shelters is not sufficient for a greedy culture in light, or a stage of growth.

The poor lighting caused by several factors (the latitude, of course, the materials used to cover the greenhouses, the shaded areas) may require the installation of additional lighting.

This additional light is desirable for plants with high added values (in multiplication greenhouses, with young plants cultivated with a higher density) and plants reacting positively to a light supply: this is the case for example, for certain annual plants such as sage, cosmos, dahlia, nigella. Others, like lobelia, do not take advantage of this lighting to produce more plant material.

The auxiliary lighting is used in winter in the countries of Northern Europe, Canada, to establish a sufficient level of lighting and to supplement the natural light. This artificial lighting makes it possible to replace variations in natural light and to produce better quality plants earlier. For example, the production time of sage can be reduced by one month, using photosynthetic lighting. This saves precious space for another culture.

The light gain provided by the auxiliary lighting must be observed on the plants: the plants are bushier, with shorter internodes, and are more vigorous.

LAMPS UNSUITABLE FOR PLANTS

Many lamps are unsuitable for plants. Lamps are an essential element in hydroponics or for indoor growing more generally. So some lighting should be avoided in the use of a hydroponic system for several reasons.

Indeed, various parameters are to be taken into account such as the light intensity, the light spectrum, the cost of use ratio and of course, finally, their impact on the environment! Incandescent lamps (classic and halogen)

More than lighting, heating! As the name of the lamp indicates, light is created by incandescence, which is to say by radiation in the visible spectrum of a material subjected to the action of heat.

The tungsten filament contained in the bulb is heated to incandescent by the passage of electrical energy, which emits visible light. The rest of the energy is radiated in the form of infrared: heat!

It is not possible to grow a plant using a lamp with these characteristics. The weak luminous flux, combined with the absence of blue radiation in the luminous spectrum, gives puny plants which wither (sting). You will never see plants with such large internodes!

However, it can still find its place in cultural spaces for the management of photoperiodism. Plants receive this "light signal" of low power in sequences (or continuous), which is enough to keep them in vegetative growth. Incandescent lamps withstand cyclic use (on / off), better than fluorescent tubes and high-intensity discharge lamps.

"Halogen" lamps are incandescent lamps with halides added to emit whiter light. The bulb is made of quartz glass to withstand high temperatures. The light output of these halogen tungsten filament lamps is as poor as that of its conventional cousin.

Low-pressure sodium lamps

Despite its high light output (200lm / W the highest), this lamp is not used in horticulture. The spectrum of the emitted light consists of a band of yellow/orange colors (around 589 nm). The spectrum of the lamp is said to be monochromatic.

So, no blue light that could shorten the internodes! It is unsuitable! The gas contained at low pressures in the discharge tube is a mixture of neon, argon, and sodium. Like its pressurized cousin, HP, this lamp is used in public lighting.

Astronomical observation centers impose the use of these lamps on their close environment (roads), in favor of any other lamp for the simple reason that the light emitted is composed of very few different waves. This light is easily "eliminated," thanks to optical filters adapted to allow better observation of the sky. It is perfectly unsuitable for hydroponics!

High-pressure mercury vapor lamps

The high-pressure mercury lamp is the first high-intensity discharge lamp created. This lamp requires ballast and a capacitor to operate.

(There are however mercury lamps with integrated ballast from 160W)

The bulb, which contains a mixture of argon and mercury vapor, emits a cold light of 4300K.

The light spectrum emitted by the mercury lamp is made up of ultraviolet light that a fluorescent powder converts into visible light.

We also find these lamps with an integrated parabolic reflector, which do not have this coating converting UV into visible light. Be careful with this type of lighting, don't forget your sunglasses to protect your eyes.

These lamps were (and still are) used for lighting plants (cuttings, seedlings), but the low light flux does not allow an adult plant to grow.

This lamp will soon be abandoned because of its low light output: between 36 and 58 lm / W., The mercury vapor lamp is replaced by metal halide or high-pressure vapor lamps. It was used in road networks and lighting in shopping centers, restaurants, airports, etc.

Climate management: air renewal and circulation for humidity control

How to manage humidity in a growing space?

Climate management: The renewal and circulation of air for humidity control

The indoor growing space is subject to the constant production of humidity due to the water vapor evacuated by the plants.

To maintain the humidity of a room at a constant rate, it is first necessary to stir the air mass to homogenize it.

Then, it will be necessary to expel this water contained in the air out of the cultivated area.

Besides, the chemical composition of the air has been modified, with a reduction in the carbon dioxide content.

The renewal of stale air with healthy air helps to establish optimal plant growth conditions. (CO_2 content in the air and hygrometric rate adapted to the species, the growth stage.)

The different ways to renew the air of a culture shelter and reduce humidity:

Natural ventilation:

This method uses natural convection to replace air. It is the opening of the windows in a production greenhouse (these are the moving parts of the roof used to manage temperature, humidity, CO2 level), or a window, for small cultivated areas. The stale air, hot and humid, less dense than the cold air from the outside, is driven out of the culture enclosure.

The quality of the renewal of the atmosphere is variable because it depends on several factors (difference in temperature, humidity, wind speed, and turbulence). The opening of the growing space to the outside constitutes a gateway for insect pests.

This ventilation method is used in the professional sector, in conjunction with air circulation and / or an increase in temperature (forced air heating)

Dynamic ventilation:

Machines are used to extract humid air. It uses aerators or air extractors. These are characterized by the volume of air they move.

This material has the advantage compared to natural ventilation to offer a constant renewal of air (determined extraction rate) and better "drying power".

Controlling the humidity level is, therefore, easier and more effective with this material.

The different models of extractors for indoor gardens:

- Fans for circular ducts: extractor / intractor
  This type of fan is very common in grow rooms because they offer many advantages:
- They are easy to install; they can be fixed in any position.

- The motors fitted to this equipment are adjustable, the airflow is therefore variable
- They are compact, light thanks to a plastic scroll

CENTRIFUGAL FANS.

These extractors are also called snail aerator, for their characteristic shape, (not for the speed at which the engine turns).

This type of aerator is as efficient as the first but is less silent. A soundproofing enclosure is often offered to reduce noise during the operation of the device.

This aerator is placed directly on the wall, with the square section against it. The air is thus directly evacuated to the outside.

A wall connection (circular) installed on the other side of the wall allows the air to be evacuated outside the culture shelter via a circular duct.

The electric consumption of this type of extractor is 48W for $250m^3$ of air moved per hour, a little more greedy than the first. (RVK 125-A1 model: $220m^3$ for 31W)

The operating time of the extractors depends on the CO_2 content, the temperature, but also on the humidity. These must absolutely work when the temperature and humidity are excessive. A small rise in temperature helps to evacuate moist air masses.

It is possible to maintain the relative humidity of a culture chamber thanks to a hygrostat. This sensor measures the humidity level and triggers ventilation. Some models allow ventilation and heating to be controlled at the same time.

When the temperature is optimal or low in the culture space, it is the air blower that is responsible for reducing the humidity. But in any case, air extraction is necessary to obtain an acceptable CO2 content.

Air fans

Air extractors are used when the temperature and humidity are excessive.

The ventilators have a different role from the extractor. They homogenize the atmosphere of plants by convection of the air mass.

Indeed, there are differences in temperature and a fortiori humidity in the volume that constitutes a culture shelter. These differences are explained by the orientation of the growing space (the northern part will be wetter), the density of the plant, the presence of nutrient solution reserves in hydroponic systems, the installation of photosynthetic lighting. (temperature increase)

The air blowers will reduce the humidity thanks to their drying effects. It is a precious ally to prevent cryptogamic diseases. (They can also be a spreading agent of fungal diseases like rust by dispersing the spores)

The fans will participate in the lignification of the young plants: the frail herbaceous stems get stronger and become more resistant to insect attacks, thanks to a "wall effect."

Improper use of air blowers can have negative effects on vegetation:

- A violent airflow constantly directed towards the plants causes the stomata to close, which reduces photosynthetic activity.
- Prolonged use can excessively reduce humidity in contact with plants.

This creates a dry "environment" favorable to the development of spider mites (red spiders, aka your worst enemy).

Finally, the air brewers participate in the fertilization of anemophilous plants such as tomatoes (whose dissemination of gametes is ensured by the wind). Poor fertilization can lead to misshapen fruits.

Humidifier and Dehumidifier

Specific equipment for reducing the humidity level.

Plants generate an enormous amount of water vapor in the growing space. It is estimated that one square meter of culture can have transpiration up to 4 liters of water per day.

(It takes between 250 and 1,000 lire of water for plants to produce 1 kg of dry matter)

Indeed, it is the transpiration of water by plants that is responsible (in large part) for the circulation of the sap. It is, therefore, normal that space welcoming plants is humid.

It is a balance between the vaporization of water by plants and the evacuation of this water (or its liquefaction), which will determine the hygrometric degree. Nutrient solution tanks and plant substrate are also sources of moisture.

If, despite the aeration and mixing of the air in the cultivated space, the air is too humid for the plants, you should think of the dehumidifier. (for small growing rooms)

Condensation dehumidifier

This machine is a heat pump, a fan of which circulates the air through a heat exchanger (coil). On contact with it, the water contained in the air condenses and is evacuated (in the tank or an outlet) As it is electrical equipment (and not really economical), its use in large volumes remains limited.

The use of an absorption dehumidifier is not the panacea for growing space. This equipment operates within a determined temperature range (see manufacturer's specifications) for optimal dehumidification performance. In addition, the air that is processed by this machine is exhausted at a colder temperature. There may be a thermal shock with plants located near the device. Be careful not to transfer the problem to other factors.

Moisture absorbers:

This material uses hygroscopic materials to treat the air. Water collects in the refill before falling into the tank. The brackish liquid obtained after some time of use is to be eliminated.

This material is unsuitable for reducing humidity in a cultivated area:

- It does not allow to reach a precise or desired humidity level
- Refills of desiccant materials are expensive.

Specific equipment to increase humidity:

There are different types of equipment suitable for increasing the humidity of growing space for a small room or one hectare of the greenhouse.

As with all electrical equipment in a grow room, the use of equipment must comply with safety conditions. Water and electricity do not mix well...

Boiling humidifiers:

This material uses an electrical resistance, which brings the water contained in the tank to a boil. It is, therefore, normal for the temperature of the culture space to rise slightly.

This method of vaporization is particularly high in calories. The electrical consumption of this material is quite substantial compared to the flow.

This humidifier is particularly suitable for growing areas where the temperature is not excessive. The temperature of small gardens fluctuates rapidly with this type of material.

Winter / tropical gardens will welcome this humidifier without a problem, on the contrary.

Tropical plants (hot and humid regions) appreciate the gentle heat that is created during the spraying of water.

The most compact models have a power of 300W for a flow rate of 0.3 liters/hour.

Ultrasonic humidifiers (cold vapor)

The vaporization of water into the atmosphere by an ultrasonic humidifier uses a technique different from the first. It is the "retraction and expansion" of the ceramic cells when an electric current passes at the frequency of ultrasound that vaporizes the water, creating a mist. This nebulization of water requires little energy, much less than boiling

Humidifiers: An ultrasonic humidifier with a 4 litre tank at a power of 38W for a flow rate of 0.26 l / hour

Ultrasonic humidifiers are available with flow regulators and a hygrostat to maintain the relative humidity at the desired level. These humidifiers take care of everything

The water is vaporized in the form of a dense mist. It does not wet plant foliage as a spray of water will.

There are also ultrasonic misters that fans of vivariums know well. This equipment contributes to the decoration by recreating the dense mist, worthy of hyper humid rainforests. And of course, this must helps to increase the humidity of the environment.

Their use in small growing rooms makes it possible to increase relative humidity; however, it is more complex to maintain the air at a constant hygrometric degree: It is necessary to vary the cycles in accordance thanks to a very precise programmer.

The water that is used in these ultrasonic humidifiers must be free of minerals. These participate in the fouling of the ceramic cells. Fill the device's tank with distilled water to extend the life of the cells.

The ultrasonic humidifier is the device you need if, despite the plants, the hydroponic system, the humidity is not high enough: to be reserved for small growing areas.

Misting (Vivaria)

This system was originally designed for large vivariums (enclosures where living things are raised in a reconstituted environment, where humidity is often kept high).

This misting system is used in greenhouses and production tunnels to increase humidity, but also to decrease temperature.

Finally, we find misting devices in parks and gardens for the decorative effect and certain refreshing areas (picnic areas) or in rooms hosting green walls.

Misting contributes to the increase in humidity thanks to a high-pressure water spray in the form of fine droplets of 60 microns in the culture space.

This "finesse" of spraying gives this device great efficiency.

What is a misting system made of?

First, a high-pressure pump is required. This can go up to 15 bars in the distribution network. The sprinklers through which water comes out as a mist are mounted on the pipes.

A filter eliminates all that is likely to clog the dispensing nozzles.

In this regard, like ultrasonic humidifiers. it is best to use water with little mineral content to avoid clogging the nozzles. (Tartar deposit)

The advantage of misting is to maintain homogeneous humidity in the culture space. It can be used to combat high temperatures. This device is reserved for greenhouses and tunnels.

Continuous misting is strongly discouraged. The pump will not last long, and this will wet the foliage: it is necessary that the leaves dry before a new cycle to reduce the risk of cryptogamic diseases.

Nebulization: Fog-system

The Fog system goes even further in the finesse of the water drops. This is vaporized in the form of a mist, or the drops of a size of 5 microns are suspended in the air. We are talking about nebulization.

This device requires a high power pump to maintain sufficient operating pressure. (from 70 to 120 bars) The higher the pressure, the smaller the drops.

The cost of purchasing and installing a Fog system is quite high. In addition, it is quite heavy to set up. But it is the most efficient device. It is reserved for professionals to optimize yields. When humidity is lacking, or the heat is too high.

Indeed, it takes 600 calories to evaporate 1 gram of water. The water in suspension in the air "takes" calories from the atmosphere of the cultivated space.

It follows a change of state: (the water passes from the liquid to the gaseous), which causes the lowering of the temperature.

This device has the particularity of increasing the relative humidity without wetting the foliage of the plants.

This system is found by nebulization in multiplication greenhouses, or greenhouses hosting plants sensitive to humidity. (like cucumbers, Tomatoes during their fertilization, and we are not talking about orchids ....).

The Fog-system can be installed in greenhouses and other shelters reserved for plants; you will hear it working…

Hydrofogger

This humidifier model, designed in the United States USA, is unanimous among enthusiasts of orchids and carnivorous plants. This machine, 37cm in diameter and 48 cm in height, has a maximum flow rate of 6.6 liters per hour.

The hydrofogger still uses a technique to vaporize water in the air, without spraying water or boiling: the manufacturer explains that it is the centrifugal force exerted by a powerful motor (whose power is unknown!) Which "vaporizes »the water into the atmosphere where the plants are grown. The drops would have a diameter of 20 microns. The engine and the movement of the blades of the device generate a blowing noise of 62 decibels.

Control of thrips

Thrips in houseplants

The damage to thrips is above all aesthetic. But if present in large numbers, these insects can weaken the plant.

When the temperature is high, the thrips complete its life cycle in two or three weeks.

Three species of thrips are commonly encountered on indoor plants.

Damage

- Using their mouthparts, thrips pierce plant tissue to suck out the liquid. The emptied cells fill with air; the plant gradually covers itself with small white or silvery spots. When the spots are very numerous, they form longitudinal streaks.
- The attacked leaves and flowers may warp and wilt. The presence of thrips weakens the plant and slows its growth.
- As thrips also attack buds, new leaves and flowers may be misshapen and stunted.
- Thrips can spread viral diseases.

Screening

- Regularly inspect the underside of the leaves and the inside of the flowers. Shake the different parts

of the plant over a sheet of paper and use a magnifying glass to identify the insect.
- Sticky traps can indicate the presence of adults. Install traps near the foliage and inspect them frequently.
- Thrips, black and shiny excrement, are visible on the foliage.

Tolerance threshold: Intervene as soon as the problem is identified.

PREVENTIVE MEASURES

- Carefully inspect the plants you introduce into the house, those you just bought, and those that have spent the summer outside.
- Maintain the vigor of plants by watering them regularly.
- Disinfect cutting tools with 70% isopropyl alcohol (rubbing alcohol).
- Perform frequent screening.

Ecological control

- Isolate infested plants in a cool room.
- Trim and destroy badly damaged stems and leaves.
- Outside, dislodge the thrips with a fairly strong jet of water.
- Indoors put the plants in the shower.
- If the infestation is significant, repot with healthy soil.
- Soak one or two cloves of garlic in one liter of water for 24 hours.
- Filter the maceration and add a tablespoon of phosphate-free dish soap.

- Then spray all parts of the infested plant, until it drips.
- Repeat the treatment every five days for three or four weeks.
- Soap-based insecticides are also available commercially. Follow the manufacturer's directions.

GENERAL Plant tips

Why do plants grow in hydroponics?

The plant needs five things: light, air, water, heat, and nutrients. The light and warmth depend on the location we choose for our plants: for example, are they close to the window in a warm room or at a dark angel in the cool hallway? The choice of location is decisive for light and heat. The interplay of air, water, and nutrients, however, takes place in the planter, i.e., in the root area of the plant.

The plant not only breathes through its leaves but also has root breathing. If, for example, a crop gets too much water all the time, it always has too little air, it "suffocates". Root respiration, therefore, plays a crucial role in plant health. When it comes to air as a growth factor, hydroponics is now helping him. The expanded clay spheres are dimensionally stable and thus always guarantee sufficient air supply to the roots. These absolutely safe "air chambers" could only be displaced by too much water - that's why the water level indicator is part of hydroponics. With its display of the minimum, the optimal or maximum water level in the vessel, it ensures that we do not need water more than the plant needs.

What about water and nutrients in hydroponics?

The plant accesses its food through the water - as soon as the nutrients get into the water, one speaks of a "nutrient solution". Contrary to popular belief, plants do not get their nutrients directly from the earth but absorb minerals from the water. Outside, the earth mostly serves as a base and storage for water and nutrients. In hydroponics, the living green receives all the necessary nutrients from the irrigation water, and the fertilizer dissolved in it - so always pay attention to the special hydroponic fertilizers when shopping! This can be dosed very precisely because the expanded clay itself is inorganic and "neutral", it does not form a buffer and does not interfere otherwise.

At the same time, the water level indicator ensures that not too much is watered - this type of misunderstood "pampering" is the most common cause of plant damage. At the same time, the water level indicator tells us when the water supply has been used up and should be watered again. This creates a change like at low and high tide, which the plants get well. The plant is obviously doing well with the balanced air-water ratio in the planter. And the plant lover enjoys the luxury of significantly longer watering intervals.

The plants can thrive and always breathe at the same time with optimal water and nutrient supply. Hydroponics thus offers our houseplants three out of five growth factors in an optimal and safe system. Because this works so well and plants in hydroponics often thrive better, the system has long been used where nutrition is concerned - for example, in growing vegetables.

Culture pot - what is the correct size of the culture pot?

Culture pots are coordinated with the water level indicators and standardized in height and diameter. Hence the uniform names that indicate diameter/height, e.g., B. 13/12. When moving a plant, the new pot should be one or two sizes larger.

Lifespan - How long can hydroponic plants last? What are your biggest enemies?

Hydroponics can last for decades under optimal conditions. Systems that are older than 20 years are known from practice. The fact that many plantations fail beforehand is often due to the water level being too high or insufficient lighting conditions. In addition, serious mistakes in nutrition are still made. In individual cases, there can, of course, be a variety of other reasons for failure. Basically, it should be noted that hydroponic plants are more durable than plantings in horticultural soils based on organic substrates.

Climate zone - Which climate is particularly suitable for hydroponics? Can it also be used in subtropical hot areas?

The hydroponic system is also suitable for subtropical hot areas. High water accumulation can possibly lead to stronger effects due to lower oxygen contents. The solution is simple: keep the water levels low if necessary.

Outside greening - Can plants with lava or hydro stones or Seramis products stand permanently in the garden?

Various volcanic ash, expanded clay, and slate are suitable for greening outdoors. They can be used for beds, pots, and green roofs. For Seramis, on the other hand, only one example is known so far in which the outside greenery has proven to be frost-resistant.

Sun protection glazing in the winter garden

In the winter garden of my parents-in-law, several plants take care of themselves both in hydroponics and in Seramis, although to my knowledge, there were no crop defects with regard to light, water, fertilization. The relative humidity is often below 40%, rarely does it rise to 50%. It is a fully heated winter garden with underfloor heating, automatic ventilation, and shading, as well as sun protection glazing.

Low humidity is not uncommon in a heated winter garden, where the plants are in individual containers and are not planted in beds. With an adequate water supply, this is well tolerated by the plants. The problems described may be related to the glazing of the winter garden.

Sun protection glazing filters out the blue and red wavelengths of light that are important for plants. The plants are in the dark, although it is bright for the human eye. The result is considerable growth disturbances, and in extreme cases, the plants die off. This problem was examined by the technical consultant Dieter Jansen and described in various publications

Is it possible to grow hydro plants from fruit seeds yourself? Specifically EG. Avocado, mango, coffee, or coconut. What do I have to take to care of?

Of course, plants can be propagated from seeds for hydroponics. It is optimal if this happens in an inert substrate. Propagation substrates must, however, be finer-grained than the subsequent culture substrate so that the seed can absorb sufficient moisture and does not dry out. You can use Perlite, Seramis, or expanded clay with a grain size of 2 - 4 mm. Coarse sand is also possible. Cultivation in small rockwool cubes is particularly good.

Water level - I have equipped my new apartment with mostly small hydroponics. Unfortunately, I had to find out that all the plants gradually get brown leaves or parts of the plant are hanging. The hydro plants stand on granite window sills above the heater. Is that the reason for the death?

A location directly above the radiator is certainly not the best. But did that cause the damage? –The description of the symptoms is more reminiscent of culture that is too moist, for example, too high a water level. Easily recognizable from the fact that the roots have rotten. The small vessels you mentioned are particularly susceptible to this. The cultivation of plants in hydroponics in vessels with a pot height of only 9 cm or less is very problematic.

ROOTING

GROW YOUR OWN HYDRO PLANTS

Expanded clay - I got the tip of a rubber tree that is already growing in hydroponics as an offshoot (about 50 cm long). I was advised to put the offshoot in water for rooting. That was two weeks ago. However, there are still no roots. Should I rather put the offshoot in fine-grained expanded clay? What should I watch out for?

Rooting rubber trees is not easy. For this reason, it is recommended to "peel off" the plants. The shoot to be rooted is left on the mother plant, and a notch is cut out only up to about half of the stem. The whole thing is then covered with wet peat garbage and a film and waited until roots have formed.

Then the shoot is completely cut off from the plant. In your case, you should wait for roots to form in water. To do this, place the container as warm and bright as possible and be patient. It will certainly take a few more weeks. Change the water weekly. A weak fertilizer solution can be helpful. Use about 1/10 of the usual concentration of liquid fertilizer.

Plant seeds - can I also spread plant seeds on hydroponics? If so, what do I have to consider? What is rock wool?

Sowing for hydroponics needs fine granules. Sowing will hardly be possible in the normal expanded clay of 8/16 mm grain. In practice, farms are usually sown in perlite. It is white volcanic ash that is also used as insulation in the construction industry. Alternatively, you can also use Seramis for sowing. If possible, cover the seeds Slightly with granules so that they do not dry out and set up at the best possible temperature. Do not cover "light germs".

Stone wool - is it better to root cuttings on expanded clay or stone wool? Can you successfully continue cultivating cuttings rooted on rock wool on expanded clay?

Experience has shown that cuttings in rockwool form roots better and faster. This may be due to the better contact between the cutting base and the substrate, which results in a better water supply. Young plants rooted in rock wool can be converted into expanded clay relatively easily. Before the plants are rooted in the expanded clay, however, an adequate water supply must be ensured. The rockwool cube must not dry out during this time. Later drying out of the cube is definitely desirable.

Water

Watering **hydroponic systems** : Please water the plants only up to the optimum mark. To do this, only pour tap water from above onto the expanded clay surface. Coffee, tea or cleaning residues lead to plant damage and unpleasant smells. The next pour is only necessary when seeds level shows the minimum. Let the plant stand at this level for three days and only then water it again with fresh water. The water level must be low in between as plant roots need air.

If there is a permanent lack of oxygen due to a constantly high water level, root rot threatens.

Tip: Gently knock on the water level indicator as a check or tilt the vessel slightly to the side.

Watering rhythm and amount of water vary depending on the size of the container and plant, as well as the location and ambient temperature.

Flushing through - I have two hydroponic plants that are so large that I can no longer flush them out in the bathtub (tendril on the stump about 2 m high and tied to the wall). Then what do I do?

In the meantime, the recommendation to flush the vessels has changed. This only makes sense in the event of an acute error (over-fertilization, contamination of the nutrient solution with beverage residues, etc.). As a rule, this can be dispensed with.

Rainwater - I water my hydro plants with rainwater. Which fertilizer can I use to achieve the best nutrient supply?

The use of rainwater to irrigate plants indoors, regardless of whether hydroponics, Seramis or peat culture, is not without problems. This is due to the fact that the fertilizers offered in retail are not suitable for combination with salt-free irrigation water. The explanation is complex: The use of ion exchange fertilizer (Lewatit HD50) requires a certain amount of salt in the irrigation water so that the ion exchange works.

Lewatit HD50 should be suitable for all degrees of water hardness, but the manufacturer recommends adding lime to soft water / rainwater. The ion exchanger binds almost all of the calcium, magnesium and sulfate, so that the plants lack these essential nutrients.

Liquid fertilizers are mistakenly seen as an alternative for low-salt irrigation water. But they are also not suitable for this area of application. Liquid fertilizers do not contain any significant amounts of calcium and magnesium. For technical reasons, both nutrient elements cannot be contained in concentrated stock solutions. In addition, liquid fertilizers contain comparatively high ammonium-N proportions, which in combination with low-salt irrigation water lead to a sharp drop in the pH of the nutrient solution,

That is why we offer "Lewatit for soft water", which is already mixed with lime.

Oxygen content - Can you improve growth by enriching the irrigation water with the help of an air pump or with oxygen tablets?

Freshly poured irrigation water is usually almost saturated with oxygen. A further oxygen supply will therefore have no effect. There is no experience with oxygen tablets (from the aquarium?). We have never had such a problem in our daily business.

Water hardness - pH value - Our water (Essen / Ruhr) has high pH values (7.2 - 7.9) with the lowest degrees of hardness (max. 1). What is the optimal fertilization for such conditions?

The pH of the irrigation water must not be overestimated. It not only depends on the water content of hydrogen carbonate ions (acid capacity or carbonate hardness), but is also significantly determined by the CO_2 content of the water. In the case of soft, weakly buffered water, the pH value is very strongly influenced by small influences, both upwards and downwards, without this being of any importance. The decisive factor for the plant is the pH, which is set after the addition of fertilizer. In the short term this is mainly determined by the phosphate concentration (phosphate buffer system) and in the medium and long term by the mineral nitrogen form (ammonium or nitrate).

We recommend our "Lewatit for soft water", which is already mixed with lime.

Water temperature - In my 20 year old Strelizie I found that the water temperature was significantly above room temperature. What can be the cause and are there negative consequences?

A higher nutrient solution temperature in the vessel compared to the room temperature can usually be caused by two reasons: influence by heating (radiator or floor heating) or by direct sunlight. If necessary, the vessel can be protected against the influence of the heating by an insulating layer (polystyrene pad, etc.).

If the vessel is exposed to direct sunlight, this has a particularly strong effect on dark vessels. Whether the temperature increase leads to plant damage depends not only on the temperature, but also very much on the type of plant. However, I am not aware of the sensitivity of Strelizien. Temperatures above 40 ° C should definitely be avoided.

EXPANDED CLAY

Questions about expanded clay

Renewal - Do you have to renew the expanded clay at some point and if so, at what intervals?

A key advantage of "hydroponics" is that the expanded clay substrate is permanently structurally stable. It is not decomposed by microorganisms, nor does it dissolve in any other way. For this reason, an exchange of the expanded clay is not necessary and also makes no sense. An exchange can only be considered for the top, non-rooted layer, if possible salt deposits have made the expanded clay unsightly.

Use - Should hydrostones be rinsed with clear water before use? Do not cleaned or cleaned stones affect the pH of the water?

Expanded clay can be rinsed with water before first use. This removes the adhering fines (dust from abrasion). Good expanded clay is subjected to regular quality control. This quality can be used without rinsing. This also applies to the pH value: expanded clay that meets the quality criteria has a small, temporary influence on the pH value of the nutrient solution in the vessel.

Grain size - Which grain size of expanded clay granulate must be used for which plants? Does that depend on the plant height or also on certain properties of the plant? Do different grain sizes have different properties or is it just about the look?

Expanded clay is commercially available in grain sizes 4/8 and 8/16. For special purposes, such as the propagation of plants, the grain size 2/4 mm is also used. The specification 4/8 means that the grain size is between 4 and 8 mm. Numerous tests have shown that the best growth is usually achieved with the 4/8 mm grain.

Nevertheless, the grain size 8/16 has established itself today, and not only for visual reasons: strong growth is not desirable in the interior greenery. The main thing here is good durability of the plants. The risk of waterlogging and the associated lack of oxygen is significantly lower with the coarser grit 8/16 and therefore preferable to the grit 4/8.

Care - Can I just wash and reuse clay pellets that have salt deposits or are their capillaries blocked?

Used expanded clay can be reused after repeated, thorough watering and rinsing. The beads can be soaked in the water for several hours. Depending on the type of adhering salts, these can be dissolved more or less easily. The sedimentation of lime and plaster is a bit persistent. Rainwater has a particularly good dissolving power because it can absorb a lot of salt.

Root and plant residues should be removed as completely as possible, as these could rot. If the old expanded clay is too rooted, it is better to take new ones.

Quality - When I wash fresh expanded clay, some clay balls do not float to the water surface. Is it advisable not to use these beads?

You can use them without hesitation. In the production of expanded clay, the clay is burned at a very high temperature of around 1200 ° C. This creates a ceramic that is largely closed on the surface. The expanded clay can absorb almost no water indoors. Depending on the proportion of trapped air pores in the expanded clay, expanded clay granules may float in water. The actual task of the expanded clay water - leading upwards on its surface - remains unaffected.

Salinization - Can there be salinization of the expanded clay? Is this then accompanied by over-fertilization of the plants?

A hydroculture vessel is a closed system. Salts entered into the vessel that are not absorbed by the plant collect. This applies to nutrient salts as well as ballast salts, which are not required by the plants or only in small quantities. In order to assess a possible risk, one has to observe what happens to the excess salts.

Basically, the capillary movement of water from bottom to top also causes the salts dissolved in it to be transported. As a result of the evaporation of water in the uppermost dry expanded clay layer, these crystallize out as a white coating. Only phosphorus is precipitated in the lower area. The deposition of the excess salts in the top layer is positive, since this leads to constant disposal and prevents over-fertilization. The plants have no disadvantage due to the salt enrichment because they do not form roots in this dry area.

FERTILIZING - AS VITAL AS EATING

Liquid fertilizer - slow release fertilizer

Liquid fertilizers are more or less highly concentrated nutrient salt solutions. The nutrients administered are immediately available to the plants. Various nutrient salts such as ammonium nitrate, potassium nitrate and ammonium dihydrogen phosphate are dissolved in water. Easy dosing is an advantage for the user. It only has to be measured according to the instructions for use and diluted with the specified amount of water. All you need is a measuring cup. The bottle cap is usually used as a measuring cup. Attention:

The dosage of different liquid fertilizers can be very different. It is always advisable to follow the instructions for use carefully.

Slow-release fertilizers contain at least some of the nutrients in a form that is not immediately available to the plant. Rather, they first have to be mobilized, i.e. converted into the form that plants can absorb. At Lewatit, for example, this is done by exchanging with the salts in the irrigation water.

What distinguishes a hydroponic fertilizer from other fertilizers?

Hydroponic fertilizers should meet the special conditions of hydroponics. These result from the lack of buffering of the hydroponic system and from the fact that it is a closed system. Important consequences are therefore: Hydro fertilizers should not contain any ballast salts (sodium, chloride, etc.).

The ammonium-N content should not make up more than about 50% of the total N supply, so that the nutrient solution does not become acidic. Exception: very hard irrigation water. The phosphate content should be significantly lower compared to fertilizers for earth culture. The copper content can be lower since copper is hardly specified. In addition, hydraulic fertilizers often contain particularly high-quality iron chelates, some of which justify the higher price of such fertilizers.

Long-term fertilizers - Is there also a rating for long-term fertilizers?

For hydroponics, only so-called ion exchange fertilizers can be considered as long-term fertilizers. For many decades the "Lewatit HD5" ion exchange fertilizer was the only ion exchange fertilizer on the market. It was developed by Bayer AG in the 1970s and marketed under various trade names. Later the same company developed the "Lewatit HD5 plus" for low-salt irrigation water (soft water).

In the meantime, only the well-known Lewatit HD50 is manufactured. This should be optimized for every degree of hardness of the water. However, the manufacturer still recommends adding lime to soft water to ensure the supply of the important calcium. For this purpose we have our "Lewatit for soft water" on offer.

Quality - can you use any liquid fertilizer offered?

The range of liquid fertilizers has now become almost unmistakable. In addition to liquid fertilizers for professionals in larger containers, products in smaller bottles are available for the hobby sector. Most of them are so-called universal fertilizers. However, some manufacturers also offer special fertilizers for hydroponics.

Many, mostly cheap liquid fertilizers do not contain trace elements. Others contain too much sodium and chloride. Composition and recommended use are very different. Therefore, be especially careful with cheap products, because trace elements are comparatively expensive.

Water accumulation - what do you mean by water accumulation during fertilization?

When growing plants in expanded clay, it is necessary to provide the vessel with a supply of water or, better, nutrient solution, since the expanded clay itself, unlike Seramis, cannot store any significant amounts. This water supply is located in the lower substrate area and is called water accumulation. With a vessel height of 19 cm, it is a maximum of 4-6 cm.

www.ingramcontent.com/pod-product-compliance
Lightning Source LLC
Chambersburg PA
CBHW071624150726
48000CB00004B/1879